THE LAST KEEPER AT SPLIT ROCK

The Last
Keeper
at Split Rock

Mike Roberts

To: Gert.

Keep the Light Shining.

Best Wishes.

Mike Roberts
July 3, 2010

North Star Press of St. Cloud, Inc.
St. Cloud, Minnesota

ISBN: 0-87839-355-2
ISBN-13: 978-0-87839-355-8

First Edition, June 2010

Printed in the United States of America

Published by
North Star Press of St. Cloud, Inc.
P.O. Box 451
St. Cloud, Minnesota 56302

www.northstarpress.com

Dedication

I dedicate this book to the U.S. Coast Guard personnel of the past, present, and future. They are the ones who stand the watches, scrape and paint the aids to navigation, monitor the radios, log the daily happenings and go out on yet another boat patrol for search-and-rescue missions. Their dedication to their fellow man, "Coastie" or civilian, is pretty much unsung, and without fanfare but when the call to service comes, they always answer it.

Acknowledgements

I WOULD LIKE TO ACKNOWLEDGE the people who helped make this book possible. My enlistment in the U.S. Coast Guard in 1966 has had a great effect on my wife, Mary, and I and our life together.

To my wife, Mary, each time it came to move to the next duty station or job opportunity, Mary cheerfully labeled and packed our belongings into moving boxes without complaint. She was and still is the adhesive that has kept our lives together through the last fifty years. She has always been my best friend, cheerleader, coach, life's partner, and companion. I hope that it will remain so and always will be.

To the many people who were stationed at the Duluth Life Boat Station during my tenure there.

To the three officers-in-charge while I was stationed at the Split Rock Lighthouse, those being:

Leon T. Woodard and his wife, Doris, and their two darling little children, Terry and Sheryl. They were our next-door neighbors, who were very caring people, and we always thought of their kids as our own. Doris sent many photos of their time at the lighthouse and was most generous with sharing her permission and knowledge with me when I was writing this book. Even though Leon has passed away, his generosity, kindness, and humor will always be remembered.

Bruce and Kathy Robb, who shared their interest, kind words, recollections of timelines and permission to use their pictures for the book.

Jim and Carole Schubert, while only being stationed there just a few months before the lighthouse was closed, have shared their stories and pictures with permission to use them, helped recall dates and event happenings of our Split Rock Lighthouse experience and our friendship over the years.

To all the Coastguardsmen stationed at North Superior Life Boat Station in Grand Marais, Minnesota, during my tenure there.

To Mike Gehm of Sturgeon Bay, Wisconsin, for his friendship and good humor during our enlistment. We were stationed together at the life Boat Stations of Duluth and Grand Marais. He was a couple of weeks behind me in boot camp and his service number was one digit more than mine. He kept everyone on an even keel at both places when things got a little tense at times. His wife, Mary, and my Mary are very compatible, and we have kept in contact over the last forty years, even going for a visit from time to time.

To Sharon Eberhardt Schulte, the author of *The Children Remember: Stories of Minnesota Children during World War II* for helping me to stop procrastinating and take the needed steps to get my book published.

To Seal Dwyer and her mom, Corinne, from North Star Press of St. Cloud, Inc., for having the foresight to recognize that there would be readers for such a book and the patience to answer the many questions of a novice and aspiring writer who knew nothing of the process of publishing a book.

To Lee Radzak, the Split Rock Lighthouse site manager for the Minnesota Historical Society for his interest in the preservation of the Split Rock Lighthouse for all of the future generations to visit and his willingness to keep me in the loop of Split Rock happenings over the years.

To all of the many visitors over the years that has made Split Rock Lighthouse one of the most visited lighthouses in the world.

Many thanks to all of the afore-mentioned people who have contributed in one way or another to my U.S. Coast Guard enlistment experience and to the Split Rock Lighthouse story in particular. It has been an interesting experience.

TABLE OF CONTENTS

INTRODUCTION

Aт THE URGING OF MY WIFE, Mary, and our three sons, Mark, Eric, and Tim, I started to write the stories of the Split Rock Lighthouse and my four years of service in the U.S. Coast Guard on Lake Superior. The writing of the book did not come as a sudden flash of inspiration but as many small contributions over a long period of time. Our first grandchild, Lilly, was born in 1999, and we wanted to leave a written record of some of our life's experiences so she and the rest of our grandchildren: Zander, Griffin, Faye, Riley, Maggie, and Cecelia, could learn something about their grandparents and how they lived their lives.

My father, Frank O. Roberts, died at the young age of forty-three in 1954, and Mary's dad, Louis J. Fodor, passed away at fifty-three in 1969. Our children never got to know either of their grandfathers. With this family history of the males dying young, I wasn't too sure I would be able to orally share the stories of our lives. With the Split Rock Lighthouse stories, I had hoped to pass onto the future generation, the trials, tribulations and life's experiences of a time long past but hopefully not forgotten in a place that was regionally prominent, much visited and historically significant.

I had been writing the stories about our time at the Split Rock Lighthouse for about ten years when I saw an advertisement in the local senior citizens newsletter on "How to Get Your Book Published." It was taught by Seal Dwyer of North Star Press. I enrolled and was fascinated as she explained the book publishing process. I brought in some of the stories and asked her if she thought a book might be in there somewhere. She said there was a great story of a regional happening with great appeal that should be told. I am by nature a procrastinator and did not act on putting the stories together until a couple of years later in the fall of 2009, when, at a book signing for classmate Sharon Eberhardt Schulte's book, *The Children Remember*, she wrote, "I'm glad we had the writing class together. I hope you produce a book soon." My thought process was, "If not now, when? I'm not getting any younger." That book signing event ended my procrastination.

The publishing of this book has unintentionally coincided with the Split Rock Lighthouse Centennial in 2010, a Minnesota-wide celebration of the founding of one of the most visited and beloved lighthouses in the world. It is my pleasure to share my story with you and hope it gives an insight to what it was like to be the last keeper at Split Rock.

CHAPTER ONE

ENLISTING AND GOING TO BOOT CAMP

BEFORE GOING INTO THE SERVICE
January 1966

"AFTER YOU PASS YOUR PHYSICAL, you have twenty-one days to get your affairs in order. Then you will be inducted." *Wow! What did Mrs. Ellefson, the draft board clerk at the Ely City Hall, just say? I'd have twenty-one days to get my stuff together, then I'd be drafted? This was a life-changing event about to take place. How did this happen to me?*

On July 25, 1964, Mary and I were married at Holy Cross Church in the Delray Section of Detroit. I was working at Ford Motor Company's Rouge Plant in the gray iron foundry on Miller Road in Dearborn, Michigan. In January of 1965, I graduated from the Plumbing and Pipefitting apprenticeship while working midnights in a heating and cooling unit there. I didn't much care for the big city, so I quit my job, and Mary and I left Detroit for Ely, Minnesota, in April. We lived at my mother and stepfather's home in Winton for about six weeks until we bought a ten-by-fifty-foot Vindale mobile Home in Aurora and moved it to Ely. We had purchased eighty acres in the White Iron Lake Area on Highway #1 about half a mile west on the Esterberg Road.

I found work in the end of April with Preblich and Dubbin Plumbing and Heating in town and worked for them until I got laid off in the early fall due to lack of work. I was hired by the construction company, Huncan, Arundel and Dixon to help reline the cement silos used to store and ship crushed taconite from the nearby Reserve Mining Company. The silos were about 120 feet high and lined with steel railroad track spaced about eight inches apart. The rails stopped the wear on the inside of the silos as the rock, delivered on a belt from the crusher, fell into the loading position. Railroad cars were loaded as the train slowly drove beneath the silos. When the cars were full, a locomotive hauled them to Silver Bay for further processing into taconite pellets used in making steel.

On September 20, 1965, I was hired by Reserve Mining Company and promised a job as a pipefitter, but I was required to work on labor for thirty days before they would put me on the job I was hired for. In the meantime, the pipefitter job was filled by someone else. I applied for a Diesel Mechanic apprenticeship and was accepted for that program. The Vietnam War was heating up at that time, and the talk around work was the war, the draft, and military service. Guys were getting drafted and leaving for the service.

Out of curiosity, I stopped in at the draft board office in the Ely City Hall one day after work. I had been on a deferment as a pipefitter/plumber on my previous Ford Motor Company job as it was a critical civilian skill. However, I was no longer working in that trade. Prior to September of 1965, a married man was not subject to the draft, but President Lyndon Johnson rescinded that order and replaced it with a new one stating that all married men without children could now be drafted. When I talked to the little old gray-haired lady behind the draft board clerk's desk, I told her who I was and asked what my draft status was. She went to a filing cabinet. After shuffling through some files, she came back, gave me a big smile and said if I passed my physical, I'd be in the next bunch of men to be drafted. You could have knocked me over with a feather. I just hadn't expected that answer.

A couple of weeks later, I got my notice in the mail. It said I must report to the Federal Building in Minneapolis for my pre-induction physical. On the appointed day and time, I boarded a bus in Ely for the Cities and on our way, we stopped and picked up more guys until there was a total of four busloads of men going to take their physicals or being drafted into the service. That night we partied as we were all in the same situation. We woke up with hangovers, but after breakfast, we made our way to the Federal Building.

The place was filled with all kinds of people from all over Minnesota with uniformed soldiers telling everyone what to do. They lined all the guys who were going into the service on one side of a long hallway, and the guys who were going for their physical on the other side. When we were all lined up to the Army leader's satisfaction, he told the inductees to count off by tens, so they went down the row having them count from one to ten as they pointed at them. At ten, they had them start over again until everyone was assigned a number. After all of the men to be inducted finished counting off, the soldier in charge told all of the tens to take one step forward. The sergeant in charge said, "Congratulations, gentlemen. You are now in the Marine Corp."

Whoa! What the blazes is going on here? The Marines? My first cousin, Marty Christnagel, from Detroit, just got out of the Marines in the early 1960s. He told me the only thing he learned from them was how to kill people. I definitely did not want to go there. I could maybe take my chances with the Army, but not the Marines.

I went through the physical exam and down-heartedly rode the bus back to Ely. I got the word that I had passed the physical. No surprise there. That meant another visit with the draft board lady.

She again said after I got my draft notice, I had twenty-one days to get my affairs in order, and then would be drafted. What to do? What to do? I didn't want to take my chances with the Marines as they were sending guys right out of boot camp to Vietnam. I had worked with a guy, Clarence Lossing from Babbitt, at the mine in the Surface Maintenance department. He was drafted into the army and ended up getting killed in Vietnam.

Well, I knew I had to take some kind of action, do something in my best interest. My father had served in the Navy during World War II, and he had been married with three kids. I thought that the Navy might be the way to go. Running off to Canada as a draft dodger was definitely not an option for me. I couldn't live with myself taking that choice, even if it meant I had to go to Vietnam. I couldn't take the draft dodger to Canada route. I took a day off from work and went to Virginia and Hibbing to see some recruiters. I thought if I enlisted in the Navy or Air Force, I'd be able to use my pipefitter experience and not end up in Vietnam as cannon fodder. When talking to the Air Force recruiter, he flat-out laughed in my face and said I didn't have a snowball's chance in hell to get in. It was pretty much the same at the Navy. When talking to the Coast Guard recruiter, a chief named Vincent Palone said that there were no openings, and he had a long waiting list. As I was about to walk out the door he said, "Wait a minute. I have a recruit who signed up for April, but I don't think he will go when he's called. If he doesn't go, would you take his place?"

I said, "Yes, I'd take his place if he backs out."

Chief Palone asked me to come down to the office in Duluth to take some pre-service aptitude tests. I did and passed with flying colors. He then sent a postcard to

Mike and Mary Roberts on their first anniversary, July 25, 1965 (Photo courtesy Mary Roberts)

the draft board so they wouldn't draft me in the meantime. The guy did back out, and that opened up a slot for me.

When the time came, I enlisted in the U.S Coast Guard on April 18, 1966. We left Ely when the snow was still very high, but was melting enough to turn our gravel road into a quagmire. We had to wait until the road froze to be able to leave early in the morning to travel by car to Detroit, Michigan. Mary's family lived in Melvindale, a blue-collar suburb of Detroit near Dearborn. Mary was going to stay with her family for the three months I was in boot camp. I had signed up in Duluth but was going to Detroit as they gave me travel time to bring Mary home.

U.S. COAST GUARD BOOT CAMP
April, May, & June 1966

I FLEW FROM DETROIT TO GREEN BAY, Wisconsin, stayed over night in the local Y.M.C.A., and then met up with some other recruits from Minnesota and Wisconsin at the Coast Guard recruiter's office there. We were all sworn in at the office, and from there were taken to the airport. We boarded a plane and flew to Philadelphia, Pennsylvania, where we were met at the airport and taken to a Coast Guard station across the river in Gloucester City, New Jersey. We stayed over night there and boarded a bus for Cape May the following morning. When arriving at boot camp, we were put into a forming company until all of the recruits came together to complete the company. They shaved our heads, issued us uniforms, boxed up and mailed our civilian clothes home. We lost our former identities and were about to be forged into our new role in life. It was a lonely but exhilarating feeling.

The company I was assigned to was Delta 63. The military phonetic alphabet and a number was used for the name of each company. Each letter of the alphabet has a specific word associated with it for clarity. The letters "D" and "B" at times, can sound the same, so "Delta" stands for the letter "D" and "Bravo" for the letter "B." After going through the phonetic alphabet using a number such as "63" behind the letter, the next number is "64." They then used the whole alphabet again but change the number behind it. The companies formed in the spring of 1966 were Alpha 63, Bravo 63, Charlie 63, Delta 63, Echo 63, Foxtrot 63, and so on. That's how all of the companies at boot camp in Cape May were formed, named and given an identity.

HONOR GUARD, BOOT CAMP
Boot Camp Spring 1966

THEY LINED US UP, AND Boatswain Mate Zawawa, the leader of the honor guard looked us over. He was looking for men who were six feet tall. I fit that category, was given a try out, was successful, and then chosen as a member of the honor guard. The honor guard was a ceremonial unit that marched with special rifles, bayonets, and uniforms in parades and other events in boot camp and throughout southern New Jersey. I lived with the guys in the honor guard company in separate, special barracks but daily trained with my original company, Delta 63, all the time I was in boot camp. As a member of the honor guard, we trained and marched while everyone else was relaxing. We would precision drill two extra hours per day almost every day and used 1903 Springfield rifles with fixed bayonets. We had special shoes with large taps on them, which made a clicking noise when we marched on pavement. We wore dress blue uniforms with spats, agaulets, dickies, had Donald Duck hats and used blousing rings for our trousers.

Honor huard member, Mike Roberts in parade dress blues getting ready for a ceremony (Courtesy Mike Roberts)

Mike Roberts in parade blues with Springfield rifle with fixed bayonet getting ready for a ceremony at boot camp. (Courtesy Mike Roberts)

There were two sections of the honor guard, the top sixteen and the bottom sixteen. Each section contained, obviously, sixteen men. Everyone started in the bottom sixteen. As a man became more proficient, he could work his way up to the top sixteen. At the top, we had to perform the drill formations with precision movements. If we made mistakes, we were demoted back down to the bottom sixteen, and someone else would take that top slot. Each drill had a specific name. When the drill captain called out the name of the march or movement, every participant would take the steps associated with that particular movement. It was exacting and at times dangerous as many a chambray shirt was lanced by the bayonet of a fellow marcher during practice. I was made a member of the top sixteen in my third week of training and stayed a member of that group for the rest of my twelve-week stay at boot camp.

LINING UP IN LINES & FOOD
Boot Camp Spring 1966

In BOOT CAMP, WE LINED UP FOR EVERYTHING, for chow, for haircuts, for physical training, for classroom training. The chow line up was unique, and I never did understand the rationale for it. We marched up to the mess hall and then stood in line. The toes of our shoes were touching the heels of the guy in front of you. The guy behind had his toes touching the heels of the one in front—everyone heel to toe all the way up to the entrance doors. The only reason I can think for this odd formation only in

Coast Guard recruits standing in formation at boot camp, Cape May, New Jersey. (Photo Courtesy Mike Roberts)

Coast Guard recruits waiting in formation in the chow line. (Photo courtesy Mike Roberts)

the chow line, was that it saved space. A lot of men had to stand in a very small space. If for whatever reason, someone moved out of the heel to toe formation, you were immediately sent to the back of the line at the very end.

Boot camp food was great and for that matter, the whole Coast Guard chow was great, where ever I was stationed. There was only one rule which was posted on the wall behind the servers in boot camp mess hall. "You can take all you can eat , but you will eat all you take." They enforced this one rule religiously. There was no shortage of food there but there was no food wasted in the mess hall, ever. After chow, we marched in formation to wherever we were going or if you missed the formation, you double timed (ran) everywhere you went, walking was not acceptable for recruits in boot camp

HONOR GUARD, PARADES AND GRADUATIONS
Boot Camp, Spring 1966

THE HONOR GUARD REPRESENTED the Coast Guard boot camp at Cape May as we marched in parades throughout southern New Jersey, including Atlantic City. We were sponsored by various organizations, such as the American Legion and the Veterans of Foreign Wars posts. We competed in the drill-team division of the parade and usually placed with top honors. The honor guard drill team traveled from parade to parade in motor-coach buses provided by the sponsors, and we enjoyed doing it. After the parades were finished, parade watchers of all ages would come up to us with many kinds of questions and complements. They made us feel special as we were the Coast Guard, spent a lot of time practicing our routines, and we were the crowd favorites. It gave us

Five honor guard members on the front lawn of the honor guard barracks at boot camp before a Coast Guard ceremony. Mike Roberts is in the center of the group, third from the left.

a chance to get away from boot camp training for a while, see some of the surrounding countryside and towns of rural New Jersey and meet some of the local people.

We also performed each Friday at boot camp graduations. The recruits invited their families to come to the base and witness their completion of training. After each graduation, the trainees scattered to the four winds to begin their Coast Guard careers. It was a challenge for us to do the graduation ceremony right every time but it was a lot of fun too. The guys I marched with were a pretty good bunch and we worked well together.

MAGGOT SYSTEM OF LEADERSHIP
Boot Camp, Spring 1966

THE HONOR GUARD WAS BASED on the maggot system of leadership. In that leadership system, the lowest seniority (or most junior member of the group) was considered the lowest of the low and had absolutely no power or status. They were, as it was said many times, "lower than whale crap." Some of the upper or more senior members in this system at times were insufferable and real jerks. They made life for the lower seniority recruits a living hell. Due to this harassment, more than one guy went home because they could not stand the pressure and abuse. I had a fellow low maggot go nuts right next to me during a harassment session. This recruit, after being harassed for a long time along with me and three or four, others, let out a horrible gut-wrenching scream and fell to the deck crying and whimpering hysterically while curled up in a

Honor guard maggots during a hazing session at boot camp. (Photo courtesy Mike Roberts)

Honor guard members shining shoes and doing pushups at boot camp. (Photo courtesy Mike Roberts)

ball in the fetal position. After the medics came and hauled him off to sick bay, someone cleaned out his locker. We never saw or heard of him again. Forty years later, it still makes me wonder if he ever totally recovered from the abuse of his fellow recruits.

DEAD FLEA FUNERAL
Boot Camp 1966

AS WE WENT THROUGH THE TRANSFORMATION from civilian to military in boot camp, they trained our bodies to become physically fit so we could perform the duties required of a service member. They also worked on our minds to make us think like a military person. Most of the time this was dead serious, but then there were times when it was a lot of fun. Thinking back on all of the boot camp experiences, the dead flea funeral was just pure fun. It happened on a Sunday.

Sunday at boot camp was a day of rest. We could hang around the barracks, get our gear squared away, polish what needed polishing, write letters home, go to church and generally lay back with no pressure to perform. Visitors were also allowed on base. Except this Sunday. First Class Boatswain Mate Turner, a drill instructor, came back on base. I think the drill instructors rotated duty, and this was Turner's Sunday. Boatswain Mate first class Turner was a skinny vocal black guy who thought everyone should have some fun while at boot camp. As long as he was the leader for the day, he was going to it make fun even if it was everyone's day off. He came into the honor guard squad bay and gathered the guys around him. He asked for a flea. "What flea?" someone asked.

"The dead flea that we are going to bury today" was his reply.

There wasn't a flea dead or alive in the whole Cape May boot camp, except maybe on the commander's dog, and we had five minutes to find one. We looked high and low without any luck, but then someone came up with a dead fly and presented his trophy to Turner, who said, "Close enough." He gave the band members who lived upstairs of our squad bay five minutes to turn out with all their instruments at the ready and to assemble out on the front lawn of the barracks.

He also gave the same five minutes to the honor guard to draw our Springfield and M-I rifles from the armory located in our same building. A preacher was needed to conduct the funeral services, so Turner picked a guy named Bucher from Oklahoma City for the job. Bucher turned his shirt backwards, which gave him kind of a preacher's collar, put on a rain coat and used a the Coast Guard's Blue Jacket's manual for the bible. On his head was a Dixie cup sailor's hat. Turner put the dead fly into a match box.

When the five minutes was up, Turner got everyone in line with the band leading the parade. The preacher and the pallbearer of the dead fly came next, followed by thirty-two guys in the honor guard carrying rifles. Turner was having a ball as the director and leader of the procession. He went from front to back barking orders as to how he wanted things to go. As the precession marched through boot camp from Main Street to the practice boat davits near the multistory barracks, the band played marching songs and the honor guard marched their close order drills.

The preacher, holding the Coast Guard Blue Jackets manual to his chest in a reverent manner, and the pallbearer carrying the match box casket with the dead fly in it were in the center of this procession between the band and the honor guard. As we slowly progressed across the base toward the boat davits and past the barracks, almost everyone came out to watch with some guys hanging halfway out the windows as we marched by. The onlookers for a while weren't sure what was going on as it was Sunday, a day of rest, and here was the band and honor guard marching by in formation. After a short time, they figured it out that it was high jinx, a spoof, and started to cheer and yell encouragement as we marched by. When we got to the boat davits, Turner had some onlookers dig a shallow grave in the sugar sand. After the grave was finished, he ordered the preacher to say a few words about the "Dearly Departed Insect" in the match box coffin. When the grave-side service was completed to Turners satisfaction, he had the digging crew fill in the grave. With everyone one still in formation, he had us march back toward our barracks. By now the parade route was lined with cheering recruits and bewildered visitors. Turner got his wish. Everyone had fun, the marchers in the procession and the onlookers on the sidelines, and this broke up an otherwise boring Sunday at boot camp.

HIGH PORTING RIFLES
Boot Camp 1966

DURING COAST GUARD BOOT CAMP TRAINING, we were issued World War II M-1 Garand rifles. They were heavy to shoot, heavy to drill with, and just plain heavy. We used them on the rifle range, and they were our constant companions. When marching and performing the manual of arms, we all tried to do the best we could. Some guy's best was not always up to the standard of everyone else's. The way they made us conform in boot camp was to punish everyone for the infractions of the few. Then the many would insist on better performance from the few. How they accomplished this was to punishing everyone when one guy screwed up. One form of punishment was high-ported rifles. This dreaded term was used to describe double timing (running) with our rifles lifted high over our heads. Running with that heavy rifle was hard enough, but high porting it was ten times harder. It whacked us out. It felt like our arms weighted 100 pounds apiece, and the rifle weighed a ton. From time to time, we were all subjected to high-porting rifles and we wanted to do grievous bodily harm to who ever caused it. In retrospect, it was also a way to achieve top physical fitness and unit cohesion among the men. Another thing it did was to point out who the screw-ups were. We hoped most of the worst ones would wash out before too long. Those guys who set up the rules, regulations, and training for boot camp were pretty sharp people. They got us in shape, got rid of those people not suited for the military and made us a tight unit all at once. Living it wasn't easy, though.

HAT FULL OF SAND
Boot Camp 1966

THE TRAINING CADRE AT BOOT CAMP wanted to turn out people who were physically fit and ready for active duty. They devised many ways to accomplish this goal from 5:30 A.M. calisthenics to double timing it whenever we went from place to place while not in group or formation. The honor guard was housed in an old set of barracks that we shared with the marching band upstairs. This barracks was located quite a distance from the new multistoried squad bays of the rest of the recruits. We spent at least two hours everyday except Sunday at drill team practice where we would perform all our marching routines. First Class Boatswain Mate Zawawa was the honor guard company commander. He was a young career Coastguardsman who genuinely liked the people he was training and really wanted us to excel in everything we did, which included getting and staying in shape. Before drill practice, he'd run us, and after practice he'd do the same.

If any one screwed up in his estimation, he had a special form of running to get our attention called, "Get a hatful of sand." We would have to run through the wet and swampy marshland to get to a beach on the Atlantic Ocean beach about a mile away. We'd fill our Dixie cup sailor hats with wet sand then double time back to our barracks where he was waiting. Upon arriving back where we started from, after our two-mile-plus run, he would have us stand at attention until everyone got back as sometimes there were stragglers. He had us put the hat full of sand down on the ground in front of us and do fifty push ups with our noses touching the sand in the hat on the downstroke, while counting each push up out loud and in unison. After we were done with the pushups, he'd have us stand at attention, give us more instructions, then dismiss us. We would throw the hatful of sand in a nearby dumpster.

On a few occasions, however, someone would screw up and not do exactly what he wanted. After we dumped our hatful of sand, he would ask, "What happened to the sand. I don't see it."

When we'd say, "We just dumped it in to the dumpster" he would reply, "I haven't seen the hatful of sand. Go to the beach and get one." We had just run two-plus miles, did fifty pushups with our noses in the sand and were a bit pooped. But, we had to go back to the beach and get more sand just because someone fouled up. It was all part of the mental games the military played and the physical training we needed. I lost about twenty pounds, could do fifty pushups without a problem anytime and was able to run a lot farther that I ever could before I came to boot camp. That was the last time I was in real good shape—boot camp, 1966

UNIFORM COMPANY
Boot Camp 1966

As PART OF THE HONOR GUARD, we had other duties than just marching in formations and performing in parades and at graduations. We were assigned to guard and escorting screw-ups. When a recruit failed to follow the rules and regulations of boot camp, they would try to bring them around by placing them in Uniform Company, so they would act right and get squared away by giving them special attention. The special attention was being separated from the rest of the companies after classes and at chow. They pretty much had to stay by themselves. No one was allowed to talk to them or interact with them in any way or at any time. The screw-ups or correctees wore an upside down red Dixie cup sailor hat, red puke (ammunition) belts around their waists and red spats over their shoes. We could see them coming a long way off. They were always accompanied by a guard or escort, usually an honor guard member who carried a nightstick.

I never had chow hall duty as a guard for Uniform Company but saw the correctees every day as they ate. They needed correcting or squaring away, so everything they did was square. If they were walking, standing, eating or any thing else, it was always square. If walking, they could never go diagonal but had to make all of their corners square. When eating, they had to sit upright with a straight back and their hands in their laps. They had to ask permission to eat.

Even how they ate was choreographed. They made square motions with their hands. They would grasp the utensil in their right hand, reach out to the food on the plate, and fill the utensil and raise it straight up to mouth level but out in front of them. They would then bring the food to their mouths, insert the food, bring the empty utensil back out level over the dish, lower the utensil down to the dish, release it and return their hand to their lap as they chewed. They had to look straight ahead the whole time as they chewed and swallowed the food. They followed the same procedure with the next mouthful until all of the food was gone from their plate. They drank their beverage in the same manner.

No one was allowed to sit at their table except the guard/escort. The guard/escort accompanied the special-attention correctee everywhere. I felt sorry for these guys as some of them would be crying in front of the full mess hall as we all ate our meal. I guess it was a way for the Coast Guard to let them regain their dignity and become contributing members of the group. Usually after these guys were put in Uniform Company, they were super squared away and did well because the service had cut though the fog of their thinking. If they did not conform or do as was expected of them, after they were in Uniform Company, they were sent home in disgrace. They were then susceptible to the draft or so we were told.

Uniform Company lived in a hallway in a building near the honor guard barracks. We, as guards, had to make sure they adhered to the rules and regulations of their confinement. Some of the rules included no sitting on the bunk or talking to anyone at any time unless spoken to by an authority figure. The chief in charge of the Uniform Company was named LaGrasso, and he liked to stir things up. He would come in to the area unannounced, carrying a swagger stick, making a lot of noise and yelling at the guys, trying to unnerve them. He usually succeeded in shaking them up.

An incident happened in that hallway when I was a guard for these hapless people. Chief LaGrasso came in yelling and demanding that they give him their general orders as he harshly requested the specific number for that order. If they didn't get it correct and right then, he'd hit the aluminum shelving they were using for lockers with his swagger stick, making a loud bang. The Uniform Company pukes were scared to death of him and would be shaking in their boots as he ranted and raved. When one guy didn't get the answers right, the chief put the swagger stick behind the open front of his shelving on the wall and tipped it over in to the room. All of the correctee's worldly possessions on the shelves spilled out onto the floor, scattering everywhere and making a horrible mess. The soap powder flew from the open container and mixed with shoe polish, toothpaste, shaving gear and got all over the poor guy's clothes. The correctee, now petrified and shaking like a leaf, was given five minutes to clean up a half-an-hour mess. The chief in his loud no-nonsense voice bellowed that he would be back, so it better be clean upon his return. As he left, the chief gave me a slight wink, which made me feel a little better as I was a bit scared of him myself, and I was the guard.

The correctee now had to clean it up and in the short time allotted, an impossible task for anyone. He was sobbing as he worked because he knew he'd never get it done on time and wouldn't like the consequences of failure. The chief never came back to check on the clean-up progress, but the correctee got it done. I believe the process, as painful as it was, helped this guy cut through the fog of youth and rebellion to become a contributing member of the military or went home in disgrace. I don't know what happened to that particular sailor, as I never saw him again.

TRAINING, DREAM SHEETS, & LEAVING BOOT CAMP
June 1966

THE TRAINING I RECEIVED in boot camp was adequate but not something that could or would transfer into civilian life except for some seamanship concepts, rigging and knot tying, and the discipline. However, I did learn one good life lesson there: "Don't be first, don't be last and never volunteer." I thought boot camp was like a giant Boy Scout camp where everyone played for keeps. If a person couldn't laugh at what was going on and see it as being absolutely funny, it would screw with his head. Even though I thought boot camp was easy compared to high school football physical conditioning, it was the uncertainty of the future that would get me to thinking a lot.

A few weeks before leaving boot camp, we had a dream-sheet sign up where we would list, in rank order, the duty stations we would like to go to when we graduated. I listed Hawaii as my first choice, Alaska as my second pick, and the Great Lakes Ninth Coast Guard District as my third choice. Out of the 120 guys who graduated at the same time as I did, I was the only one to go to the Ninth District. The majority of the rest of them were shipped out to icebreakers out of Boston. After a ten-day leave spent in Detroit and Ely, Minnesota, my newly cut orders brought me to headquarters in Cleveland, Ohio, for a few days and from there, they sent me to Group Duluth. A Coast Guard seaman had drowned while on uptown liberty, and I was his replacement at the Duluth Lifeboat Station.

Mike Roberts in his dress whites in front of the 1961 red Pontiac station wagon while visiting his folks in Ely, Minnesota, while on ten-day leave after boot camp. (Photo courtesy Mary Roberts)

CHAPTER TWO

DULUTH LIFEBOAT STATION

DULUTH LIFEBOAT STATION
July through November 1966

I ARRIVED AT THE GROUP DULUTH HEADQUARTERS around the Fourth of July 1966 and was stationed at the Duluth Lifeboat Station on Park Point. My first assignment was as a crew member of a search and rescue lifeboat.

We had a thirty footer, a thirty-six footer and a forty-foot lifeboat. On weekend patrols, the boat would go out through the Duluth Entry under the aerial bridge out into the bay, head south along the sandy beaches on the east side of Park Point, go through the Superior Entry and come on the west side of Park Point back to the station. It usually took us all afternoon to make that circuit. I found this an interesting and scary kind of duty. We would rescue overturned boats and stranded boaters. I had a few adventures as a life boat crew member.

The Duluth life boat station and Group Duluth headquarters with the USCG Cutter Woodrush tied to the dock and an inbound ore carrier in the background. The photo was taken from up in the Coast Guard observation tower at the Duluth life boat station. (Photo courtesy Mike Gehm)

HIGH PAINTING IN DULUTH
July through October 1966

DURING THE SUMMER OF 1966, I was asked by Boatswain Mate first class Edgar Colbertson, the Station's Aid to Navigation officer, who was in charge of all of the navigational aids at the station, if I was afraid of heights. I told him no, which was the truth. I didn't like them very much, but I wasn't afraid of them. I was promptly made a high painter on the Aids to Navigation day markers and high structures in the Duluth Harbor, Superior Entry, and the St. Louis bay and river. I replaced Don Huntington as he was getting out of the service and going back to Minneapolis. Me and first class Colbertson were the painting crew. He'd drive the boat and requisition all of the supplies, and I'd do all the painting. The rigging equipment was tied off on the top of the structure and hung down from there. I did all my own rigging and tied all the knots, so if a knot failed or broke loose for whatever reason and I fell, it would be my own fault. The equipment consisted of a four-inch paint brush, gallons of Aklyd gloss paint and thinner, a rope fall, which consisted of a couple of multi-sheaved pulleys, and a bosun's chair. The bosun's chair was like a kid's swing, a two-by-twelve-by-twenty-four-inch board with ropes, on either side of me, threaded through two holes drilled in the board for that purpose. Like a kid's swing, I sat on the bosun's chair suspended from the pulley with a hook on it. Another pulley was tied and suspended from the top of the structure to be painted.

I started at the top and scraped and painted as I came down. Most of the day markers were from fifty to about 100 feet high—some in the water on a circular cement platform and some on land. When the boat's pilot, who was steering the ship, came into the harbor through either the Superior Entry or the Duluth Entry under the aerial bridge from out in the lake, they lined the vessel up with the day markers to stay in the center of the channel. Colbertson was the ground man, and I did all of the painting. He sat in the thirty-foot boat and watched a small portable twelve-volt TV while I worked up high. He would get me anything I needed or dropped so I wouldn't have to come down to pick it up. We painted quite a few day markers

Top: Duluth Aerial Bridge. (Photo Mike Roberts) Bottom: The swinging railroad bridge in the ship-passing or open position. The Blatnick high bridge is in the background. (Photo Mike Roberts)

that season and little did we know that it was to be Colbertson's last summer. He was killed in a rescue mission attempt on the break wall of the Duluth Entry near the aerial bridge during a huge storm. He was lifted high into the air and smashed on the breakwall by a gigantic wave that caught him and the two other men of the rescue party unaware. There is a monument dedicated to him and his life saving efforts on the north side of the ships' channel near the aerial lift bridge in Duluth's Canal Park. The huge iron gates that can be closed to block entry to the breakwall were erected after his untimely demise.

Mine was truly a boring and taxing job, scraping and painting all day long suspended in the air on a bosun's chair, so I asked for some help. They sent Ron Prie out as a relief painter, but that didn't work out. Then they sent Art Spaun to help do the job, and that worked out great. Art was a seaman from New Jersey with a thick Jersey accent. He had just come off of a Long Range Aids to Navigation Station in the Pacific Ocean on Iwo Jima, which had been the site of a huge battle with the Japanese in World War II. It was isolated duty, and Art talked about going into some of the caves there looking for relics. He was still a little nutty, as he had to stay on the LORAN station for one year before getting off the island. Art was absolutely fearless except for spiders and people. He was scared to death of spiders and was apprehensive around people, not trusting anyone very much. We got along well, pulling pranks on each other the rest of that summer. Art and I teamed up on occasion to scare the daylights out of our friend, third-class petty officer Dave Talbot from Indiana.

Some of the other guys stationed at Duluth Lifeboat Station while I was at there in 1966 were: Dave Gusky, seaman (Cleveland, Ohio); Mike Gehm, seaman, who later made third-class petty officer engineman (Green Bay, Wisconsin); Ron Prie, engineman (Milwaukee, Wisconsin); Casey Callahan, second-class petty officer, boatswain mate (Chicago, Illinois); Don Huntington, seaman (Minneapolis, Minnesota); Art Linn, yeoman petty officer (Hibbing, Minnesota); Ed Volick, engineman petty officer (Wisconsin); Lieutenant Commander Farmer, commander of Group Duluth; and Tom Sawyer, cook (Michigan). The time I spent at Duluth was long ago, my duration there was short, and I just don't recall the names of rest of the twenty-plus crewmen stationed there at that same time. They were a hardworking, fun-loving group of guys that were brought together by circumstances that, at times, were life threatening, as they answered their country's call to service.

BOAT CALLS
Summer 1966

WHILE STATIONED AT THE Duluth life boat station, I was part of a search and rescue crew. We had a rotating duty roster—so many days on and so many days off—all summer long. We worked a full eight-hour day, five days a week. We did lawn, vessel and building maintenance and aids to navigation as our major duties. We kept the place in tip-top shape, and at the same time, we served as part of a boat crew. Seven days per week, twenty-four hours per day, we were on call. There were three boats and three boat crews. One was "ready," the crew that scrambled immediately when a boat call came in on the radio or telephone.

The stern of the thirty-foot Coast Guard rescue boat leaving the Blatnik high bridge and the railroad bridge in the background. (Photo Mike Roberts)

The sailor standing watch monitored two or three radio frequencies, twenty-four hours per day, seven days a week, sounded the alarm. The standby boat crew answered the next boat call when the ready boat was on its way to a rescue mission. Then a third boat and crew was brought in, ready to go when the other two boats were underway.

Each boat had three crew members consisting of a coxswain, engineman, and a seaman. The coxswain, usually a petty officer boatswain mate, drove the boat; the en-

The forty-foot Coast Guard rescue boat heading into the Duluth Entry Ship Canal with a chief coxswain at the helm. Note the seaman standing beneath the flag in a life vest. (Photo Mike Roberts)

Superior Entry light on the end of the washed out catwalk on the break wall. (Photo Bruce Robb. Used with permission)

gineman kept the boat running; and the seaman did whatever job was needed at any given time. On the weekends, we would patrol the Duluth Harbor, go under the aerial bridge through the Duluth Entry, out past the break wall and out into the bay. We would turn south, go past the beaches of Park Point and then go back west into the Duluth harbor though the Superior Entry. We would patrol up the west side of Park Point back to the Coast Guard station.

Most of the action was on the west side of Park Point, in those days most everyone had a great deal of respect for the power and unforgiving coldness of Lake Superior. Most of the time the rescues were mundane: boats ran out of fuel or people who couldn't get their boat started. However, two rescue missions I was on stand out from all of the others: ore boats and bridges

RAILROAD BRIDGE PERSONNEL TRANSFER
Summer 1966

A BOAT CALL CAME IN, AS the operator on the moveable swing railroad bridge near the Blatnik high bridge did not answer the radio or phone. The bridge would swing out parallel to the channel so the ships could pass and then swing back into position, after the ship passed, so the trains could cross the channel. The bridge had swung out into the boat-passing position, but failed to go back to the railroad-crossing position, and there was a train on its way to cross the channel. We sped to pick up a bridge operator to relive the operator presently on the bridge who had not answered the calls. The relief operator jumped on board, and we raced to the swung-out bridge where he leaped off and hurriedly climbed the ladder to the operator's control tower. The operator who wouldn't answer the radio or phone appeared to be dead. The relief bridge operator swung the bridge back in place, just in time, for the train to cross. After the train went by, the emergency medical technicians drove the ambulance down the tracks and tried to resituate the stricken operator, but he had expired. They figured he died of a heart attack.

ORE BOAT EVACUATION BOAT CALLS
Fall 1966

THE ORE BOATS CAME INTO the Duluth harbor to load up on iron ore pellets and transport them to Gary, Detroit, or Cleveland. The taconite pellets were used to make pig iron in a blast furnace, which then could be refined to make steel. Time was of the essence as the shipping season was short. Boats didn't stay long in port. After they were loaded and headed out into the lake, they don't slow down for anything. On two separate occasions, we got distress calls from ore boats underway with their cargo heading down the lake. The first distress call was for a sailor that had a heart attack, and the second concerned a man who had broken his arm badly. Both sailors needed medical evacuations from their ships.

From on the shore, these huge vessels don't appear to be moving very fast, nor do they look that tall. However, alongside these behemoths presents a completely different image. They are very high to the top of the deck and are moving at a great speed. We pulled alongside the starboard side (right) side of the ship, and the crewmen dropped a line called a painter, which we tied to our bow. We rigged up fenders to keep our small boat from scraping the side of the ore boat. They then dropped another line, which we made fast to our stern. The two vessels were now traveling at the same speed and attached together by those secured lines.

Our forty-foot boat was like a toy compared to the ore boat. When we were alongside, it was like being tied to a building but when looking out at the water ten to fifteen miles per hours. The first ore boat crewmen lowered a stokes litter with the heart attack victim inside to our deck in the one instance. In the other rescue effort, the man who broke his arm climbed down a long extension ladder the ore boat crew lowered over the side onto the deck of our rescue craft below. We held tightly to the ladder base and they held the top. As soon as the medical evacuees were on board, in

An ore boat underway out in Lake Superior. (Photo Mike Roberts)

both instances, we cast off the lines and went at full speed back to Duluth where we were met by an ambulance that took them to the hospital for treatment. Neither ore boat slacked off speed at all during the medical transfers but kept to their schedule toward their downlake destinations.

The Coast Guard Float
Summer 1966

DURING THE SHORT TIME I was stationed at the life boat station in Duluth, we built a float. It was used for public relations purposes and was entered in all the town celebrations for miles around. It was a joint work effort by most of the guys at the station. Anytime we had some spare time, we worked on the construction of this representation of Coast Guard ingenuity. Seaman Charlie Schwab of the life boat station and Ensign Chuck from the Marine Inspection office were the planners, shakers, and movers of the project, but the guys at the station rolled up their sleeves and provided the elbow grease to make it happen.

The float was mounted on a trailer frame that was pulled behind a Coast Guard vehicle. When it was completed, the front of the ship rose up and down as if riding the waves, and every time the bow came down, water would be sprayed out from under the bow into the crowd. It didn't get them soaking wet just a little damp from the

The Coast Guard float with unidentified girls in the foreground. Note the helicopter with turning rotors on the stern of the boat. (Photo Mike Gehm. Used with permission)

spraying water. A man was hidden under the bow with a hand pump mounted on a fifty-five-gallon barrel of water, and he controlled the spray. On occasion, there was a helicopter mounted on the stern that would rise up off of the ship's deck as the rotors turned.

This award-winning masterpiece was entered in many of the local parades where it wowed the crowd. It was a source of pride for all that worked on it and was a visible symbol of a Coast Guard presence. It was the result of many man hours of team work focused on a common goal. We had a lot of fun building it and took pride in showing it off in parades through out the area.

SCARING DAVE TALBOT
August 1966

WHEN STATIONED AT THE Duluth Life Boat Station, my Coast Guard mate Art Spaun and I were always pulling pranks on one another and at time we would focus our mischievousness on other station members, too. Dave Talbot was from somewhere down in Indiana and loved to read stories about ghosts and supernatural phenomena. He was an E-4 in rank but still was just one of the guys. Sometimes rank or rate separated the men. E-3s might hang out with E-3s and E4s, but E5s usually hung out with men of their rank. Dave had to stand watch just like the rest of the lower-ranked sailors.

Standing watch was part of our daily routine, and we had a rotating duty roster. We had so many days on and so many days off. We all had to work an eight-hour day, five days per week but we also had to stand watch or be on duty as part of a search and rescue boat crew. The lifeboat station was manned twenty-four/seven, so there was always someone on duty to answer the phone, run the teletype and monitor the radios for distress calls.

Each man would stand a four-hour watch on his duty days either manning the watch shack/office, as part of the ready boat crew or as a member of the standby boat crew.

The boat crew usually consisted of three men, a coxswain (boat driver who was usually a petty officer, E-4, E-5, or E-6), an engineman, and a seaman. Whenever a boat call came in, the ready crew would scramble and get underway to affect the rescue in a very short time. In a matter of minutes, the boat was on its way to the rescue. The standby crew would take their place as the next ready boat crew and answer the next request for assistance if another call came in. We trained many hours for these events and were very good at the search-and-rescue business.

We started our day promptly at 8:00 A.M. with the flag-raising ceremony, called colors. We then went to work in training, base maintenance, aids to navigation, or any other duty that needed to be done. We had one hour off for lunch at noon (Duluth Station served the greatest meals anyone could ask for. I have never eaten so well before or since my lifeboat days at Duluth). After lunch we went back to work until 4:00 P.M. Now, if it was my turn to stand watch and I had the first watch, I worked until 8:00 P.M. When I were done with my watch, I had to stay at the station as I was a part of a boat crew. The watches rotated so I might have one day on and two days off or two days on and one day off or two days on then two days off. I still had to work all day but when I was off, I could leave the station, though I had to be back at 8:00 A.M. for colors the next day.

Mary lived uptown. On my days off, I would go home to our apartment on Third Street where she and I would spend the evenings together. However, when I was off, I was still accountable and had to stay home so I could be reached. If I went somewhere, I'd have to call the station and tell them where I'd be, as I was part of the back up boat crew. If they sent out the ready boat and then the second boat went out, they would then call the third boat crew that was off duty to come back on duty in case that boat was needed. Consequently, they wanted to know where I was at all times so they could call me back for search and rescue, if needed. It was quite restrictive and all consuming of my thoughts and actions. When I was off duty, I really wasn't off duty completely, not when I was always subject to a fifteen-minute recall to serve on a search and rescue mission.

The watches ran in four-hour increments except during the 8:00 to 4:00 work day. After the work day, 4:00 P.M. started the first watch and it ended at 8:00 P.M., the next watch was 8:00 P.M. to 12:00 midnight, the mid watch was from 12:00 to 4:00 A.M. and the next watch was 4:00 A.M. to 8:00 A.M. All the watches were pretty much the same—listening to three different radio frequencies for distress calls, answering the office phone, taking weather readings at the weather station out near the seawall and monitoring the teletype from the District and the group Duluth outlying station. The search-and-rescue stations at Grand Marais and Bayfield had teletypes—a means of station to station written communication.

After lights out a 10:00 P.M., another job was added to our list of things to do. Every hour on the hour was the fire watch inspection of the boiler room. The midwatch was from 12:00 midnight to 4:00 A.M., and it was spooky. All the lights were out, the crews were sleeping, and the place was very quiet except for the constant chatter on the radios and the clattering of the teletype as incoming messages from all over the district came in. Every hour on the hour came the fire watch, which consisted of taking a Detex clock from the watch room and walking through the hallways of the darkened and sleeping station. The path to the boiler room was out through the boat house door and across the garage and through a door into the boiler room.

After checking to make sure there was no fire and that everything was okay with nothing amiss, we had to prove we had indeed made the fire watch journey to the boiler room. How this was done was by taking the Detex clock key that was hanging on a chain near the boiler and inserting it into the Detex clock. When turning the key in the clock, it registered a mark on a paper disc inside of the clock so the supervisors could see that the required fire watch had been made within the prescribed time. It was the only key for the clock, and it hung in the same place in the boiler room all the time. If I didn't have the mark on the disc with in five minutes either side of the hour, my fanny would be grass, and the officer of the day the lawnmower. I did not want to miss a punch on the Detex clock. This was a ritual carried out by each and every watch stander from 10:00 P.M. until 6:00 A.M. and was for the safety and well being of all the personnel at the life boat station.

Many ships from all over the world came to Duluth to deliver cargos of coal, salt, steel, and other things. These same ships would take on taconite, wheat, corn, wood, or other local and regional products to be transferred all over the world. Once a Japanese crewman from one of the "salty" (ocean-going) ships fell off his ship into the harbor and drowned. We were called out, but he had sunk out of sight and couldn't be found by dragging. The Coast Guard called off the search as they knew the unfortunate sailor would come up to the surface in a few days. Sure enough, he did surface, and the Coast Guard boat crew on duty got the call. I'm happy to say I was out painting day markers, so I wasn't involved in that sad recovery.

When a body had been the water for a few days, decomposition made it, pretty ripe and rank and no one wanted to touch it. But, the body still had to be recovered. How it was handled was a Stokes litter lowered by ropes into the water under the subject and then lifted up, capturing the body in the litter. The water drained though the mesh of the litter as the body was lifted into the boat. The boat sped for shore and, after docking, the litter was again lifted and carried up the dock. The county coroner came, pronounced the subject dead and transported the body to a mortuary.

The Stokes litter, an iron pipe frame around contoured chicken wire mesh fencing formed in the shape of a very large person, had some ropes attached at both foot and head ends and both sides, so it could be lifted up when it in position under the floating subject to be recovered. After it was used, the litter was burned off to get rid of the small pieces of flesh that might be stuck to the mesh and then repainted before the next use. It's important to understand what a Stokes litter is to understand an amusing but scary incident perpetrated upon Dave Talbot by Art Spaun and me.

Dave loved to read scary Stephen King type stories while on the midwatch. He also enjoyed any other type of spooky scare-the-daylights-out-of-you tales from the crypt. Technically we weren't supposed to read while standing watch, but Dave read anyway. Who was going to catch him? Everyone was either asleep or gone, and reading made the time go by faster.

Dave was an E-4, and Art and I were E-3s, so Dave could make us do whatever he wanted as he had a higher rank. On the day the coroner came to pick up the body of the Japanese sailor, Dave was scheduled for the midwatch. He either said or did something to Art and me, which made us reply good naturedly, "Talbot, we're going to get you." Now, we didn't say what we were going to do or when we were going to do it. We weren't going to hurt him in any way, just scare the hell out of him. He said something like, "Oh, blow it out your ears. You guys don't scare me."

Art and I decided we were going to scare him that night. The boat house was a very spooky place. It smelled of old fish, water, diesel fuel, gasoline, and on this particular night, the decomposing flesh of the dead Japanese sailor as the Stokes litter hadn't been burned off yet. There was a dim nightlight in the corner up near the ceiling that cast shadows about the boat house. A person could barely hear the lap of the waves as they hit the boat house floor at the slip which at 2:00 A.M. was very scary, especially if a person was reading horror stories before going on the fire watch inspection. At about 1:50, Art and I got up out of bed, sneaked down into the boat house to find a place to hide. Art hid around the corner from the boiler and the Detex key. He put on an old mop head on his head and a foul-weather hat on top of the mop head wig. He even looked scary to me, and I knew who he was.

I crouched under a work bench concealed from Talbot's view as there was a little cubby hole between the drawers. We waited there giggling and laughing silently to ourselves. At about 1:55, we could hear Talbot coming down the hall, as he was making noise as he approached. He opened the door and entered the spooky boat house with its smells, sights, and sounds of 2:00 A.M. As Talbot started down the couple of steps to the boat house floor, he started to whistle a dry tuneless whistle to bolster his courage. He walked toward the dimly lit boiler room on the other side of the boathouse past my hiding place without seeing me and went though the boiler room door, looked around and inserted the Detex key in the clock and turned it once or twice.

When Art heard the key being turned in the clock, he flashed the light on and off a couple of times as he came around the corner, shrieking and raising his hands in the air like a monster. I, after hearing Talbot walk by, crept out from my hiding place and waited to hear the sound of the key in the clock. When I heard it and saw the flashing light, I came through the doorway to the boiler room roaring like a monster. Talbot, figuring that he was about to die, let out a horrible blood-curdling scream of shear terror. (To this day, I can still hear his scream and it makes the hair on the back of my neck stand up whenever I tell this story.) He fainted dead away and collapsed on top of the Detex clock with a thud. It wasn't funny anymore. We thought we'd killed him. Talbot was out cold. We didn't know what to do, so we thought if we splashed some water in his face he might come around. We grabbed him under his arms and started to drag him across the floor toward the water in the boathouse slip. Before we got him out the boiler room door, Talbot woke up, his eyes as big a fifty-cent pieces and his face as white as can be. He said "Ha Ha Ha. You guys didn't scare me."

We were so relived we hadn't killed him, we all started to laugh. After that incident, if Talbot tried to pull rank on either Art or me, all we had to say was, "Dave, we're going to get you," and he'd back off. It had been a heart-stopping experience for all three of us. To this day, many years later, I have not pulled another practical joke on anyone, nor have I had the desire to do so.

Third-Class BM Mike Gehm in his dress whites. (Photo Mike Gehm. Used by permission)

Playing Pool at Duluth
July through November 1966

DURING OUR OFF HOURS AS DAY WORKERS and after chow, if we were part of the ready boat crew or standby boat crew, we had to stay at the station. There was no up town liberty, so as we waited for the boat calls to come in, spending a lot of time hanging out and playing pool. We had many great games of rotation and eight ball. Mike Gehm from Green Bay, Wisconsin, brought a new game with him when he came aboard—billiards. Billiards was played on a regulation table with the cue ball and only the one, two, and three balls lined up on the spots. It was a precision game with no slop. Our next shot depended on where we left the cue ball after our last shot. We played until we lost. Mike played most of the time. He was a great billiard player and fellow crewman. After I left Duluth to go to Split Rock, he was transferred to Grand Marais and then to Devils Island Light Station in the Apostle Islands off Bayfield, Wisconsin. When I went to Grand Marais from Split Rock, he and I were stationed there together until he made third class and was transferred. I finished my tour of duty in Grand Marais and he at Devils Island. We both got out of the service about the same time and over the years, have kept in contact with one another.

CHAPTER THREE
SPLIT ROCK LIGHT STATION

MOVING TO SPLIT ROCK LIGHT STATION
December 9, 1966

I HAD ARRIVED IN DULUTH in July of 1966. Around the end of October or the beginning of November of that year, I was told that I was being transferred to Split Rock Lighthouse. In order to be stationed at Split Rock, a seaman had to be married. The man I was replacing was SN Tom Grebs from upstate New York. He was married to Ed Colbertson girlfriend's daughter, Mary, but he was getting out.

On December 9, 1966, Mary and I moved to Split Rock in the middle of a snow storm. We used the Duluth station's panel truck to haul what little belongings we had from our apartment of Third Sreet. Our new home was furnished, and we were overjoyed to begin our lives as lighthouse keepers just after Thanksgiving and a little before Christmas. It was great duty but way out in the boonies, twenty miles up the lakeshore from Two Harbors. The pay in Duluth of $98.00 dollars per month was barely enough for us to get by, so Mary had worked many jobs to supplement our income. When we got to Split Rock, they gave us money for food, and the house came as part of the deal. The Coast Guard even paid the heat and electric bill. We thought we'd died and went to heaven. How could we spend all of that money?

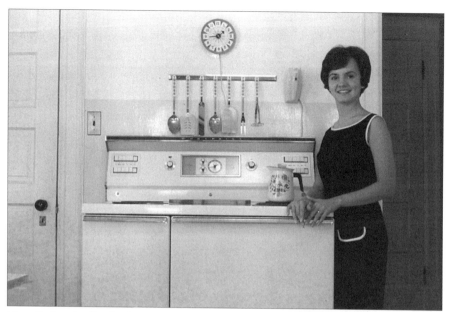

Mary Grebs standing by the electric stove in the kitchen at Split Rock Lighthouse. She was Tom Grebs's wife, the station seaman before Mike and Mary Roberts came to the lighthouse in 1966. (Photo Doris Woodard. Used with permission)

Mary and I were thrilled to be together every night and every weekend. No more boat calls or fifteen-minute recalls to the station to be part of the next boat crew called out. No more mid-watches or late night search-and-rescue missions in bad weather. We lived in the large brick two-story house, the one furthest west from the light tower. The middle house was the home of the officer in charge. The house closest to the lighthouse was empty; no one

Doris and Leon Woodard dancing in Bayfield, Wisconsin. Doris was twenty-two, and Leon was twenty-five at the time of the picture. (Photo Doris Woodard. Used with permission)

Chief Leon Woodard with his daughters: Terry (on the left) and Cheryl (right). (Photo Doris Woodard. Used with permission)

had lived there for years. The Woodards from New Bern, North Carolina, were our neighbors. Leon was the officer in charge. He was a career Coastguardsman and a first-class boatswains mate who spent his enlistments assigned to ships and shore stations.

Doris was Leon's wife. They had two darling little girls, Cheryl about five years old and Terry was three when we moved in. Leon was a very nice man who loved his family very much. His family was career Coast Guard people. I remember meeting one of his brothers who came to visit Leon at Split Rock and recall that he was stationed in Florida at the time.

In North Carolina, many young men entered the Coast Guard service with the intention of becoming career service men like their fathers, grandfathers, uncles, and cousins had done before them. Two names that come to mind when speaking of these career Coast Guardsmen are the Midgetts and the Richardsons. They are legendary families in the Coast Guard. When I was in boot camp, I remember hearing the name of Midgett as being one of the recruits who was training there at the same time. They are families who live along the Outer Banks of North Carolina and were part of the Life Saving Service before it merged with the Lighthouse Service to become the present day Coast Guard.

KITE FLYING
Spring 1967

ONE VERY WINDY DAY in the spring of 1967, I made a kite from a kit for Cheryl and Terry Woodard, and we flew it off of the cliff from our backyard. It had a real long tail as the wind gusts were so strong it was difficult to control. I eventually got the kite up in the air and gave it to the kids to fly on their own. The wind took the kite and dashed it into a tree on the edge of the cliff before I could take it back. The kids cried and cried as I tried everything to break the kite free of the tree, but it wouldn't budge. Many years later, it was still tangled in the tree as a reminder of our kite flying outing. It finally fell into the lake after the Woodard kids were grown up and long gone.

MOWING THE LAWN WITH SHIN GUARDS
Summer 1967

WE CUT A LOT OF GRASS AT SPLIT ROCK. A Jari sickle bar walk behind mower was used to cut tall grass and brush around the lighthouse. The Jari also had a snow blower attachment we used to blow snow out of the walkways. It worked pretty darn well too. It was a little underpowered for blowing a lot of snow, but it sure beat shoveling it by hand. For cutting the lawn around the buildings we had a rotary mower. The rotary had big high wheels in the back and small wheels in the front. The mower height was adjusted by moving the wheels up or down. The grass chute was located on the right side of the mower. The back of the mower deck was raised off of the ground a bit so it was easy to push.

On one lawn-mowing occasion when I was the operator, the blade kicked up a rock that flew out the back and not the side as usual and hit me squarely in the shin of my right leg. Boy, did that hurt. I shut the mower off, sat down and pulled up my pants leg to look where I got hit. I thought my leg was broken, it hit me so hard. As I sat there rubbing my shin, the impact site began to swell up. I hobbled to the house, and Mary put some ice on it, but it swelled up to a lump the size of a chickens egg before it started to go down. Before the next lawn mowing session, I found a pair of my old hockey shin guards to wear. I used those shin guards from then on every time I mowed the lawn at Split Rock. That style of mower with the large rear wheels still gives me the willies.

Leon Woodard brought up the mowing accident and the preventive measures taken by me at the next Group Duluth Safety meeting. The attending officers in charge of all the stations in Group Duluth thought it was a good injury-prevention method. They also recommended that the lawns be inspected for potential hazards before each mowing. Great advice, but I still wonder how that rock got on the lawn and why it didn't go out the discharge chute. I didn't have any long-term damage or injury but would not want to repeat that experience.

Barn Swallows Making Nests
Early Summer 1967

THE SPRING OF 1967, WHILE THE WOODARD FAMILY was still stationed at Spit Rock, swallows started to carry mud from somewhere and made it into nests under the eaves on the west side of our house. They made a lot of noise and crapped all over the place. I didn't want them there because of their racket and the clutter of their droppings everywhere. We were charged with the upkeep of the home even if it was government housing and belonged to the Coast Guard. I tried to knock the nests down with a long stick, but it was hard to reach up that high—the houses were a full two stories in height. The longer the nests were there, the more birds showed up. I had to do something, but what? They were making their nests out of mud, so I thought maybe wetting the nests would make them unable to stick to the eaves and fall down. I took a hose with a nozzle and turned it on so it had a strong stream of concentrated water. I filled the entrance hole of the nests with water and played the stream on the outside of the nest with a constant barrage. Finally the nests started to give way and fall down.

Mary, Mark, and Mike Roberts standing in the sun outside their Split Rock home on a beautiful sunny day. (Photo Mike Roberts)

The birds didn't like that very much. Just as soon as I went away, they were back, bound and determined that this was their nesting site. I would give them a little time to build them up again and would wash them away before they laid any eggs. This went on for quite a while, they building their nests and me washing them away. They gave up after many nest building attempts and went away. They must have been very smart creatures as they never came back again all the while we were stationed at Split Rock

THE SIGN AND ROCK GARDEN
Summer 1967

In the summer of 1967, Len decided that we should beautify the entrance to the station by repainting the Coast Guard sign and making a rock garden below it filled with flowers. My folks had a greenhouse business in Ely, so I got a good deal on the flowers. We planted geraniums, tuberous begonias, marigolds, salvias, and vinca

The light station sign in a rock and flower garden at Split Rock in the summer of 1967. (Photo by Doris Woodard. Used by permission)

vines. We also put some flowers near the gate to each our houses and some planters on the porches, too. We got some pipes and painted them white and put a white chain through the tops of the pipe caps with an eye. We watered the flowers daily with pride and weeded them too. It dressed the place up and said by its appearance that we really cared about the lighthouse; it was our home, not just our duty station.

ADDING A KITCHEN CABINET
Fall 1967

THE KITCHEN IN OUR HOUSE at Split Rock was old but adequate. It had the usual amenities: an electric stove, refrigerator, and sink. The sink was white cast iron and stood against the west wall. It had a single basin with a right hand drain board built in. Mary gave Mark baths in it at least once a day, but Mary mentioned that it would be nice to have a countertop and cabinet that ran from the sink to the edge of the north side wall. Doris Woodard had Leon build one for her in their quarters and maybe that's where the idea came from as Doris loved hers. I don't recall if Leon and I built it or had someone built it for us, but we put the Formica on the top.

Mike and Mary Roberts's first son, Mark, getting a bath in the sink at the Split Rock house. (Photo by Mike Roberts)

It was the first time I ever heard about or saw contact cement used. We precut the piece of Formica the exact size and dry fit it on the top of the cabinet. It fit perfectly. It was time to glue it down. We coated the top of the cabinet and the soon to be placed Formica with cement. We let it dry the recommended time called for on the can's directions then positioned it very carefully and pushed it down. It was almost in the exact place it needed to be. Just a little off. We tried to adjust it. No way. There was absolutely no adjustment possible with the contact cement. It was stuck solid and that was where it was going to stay. I was awe struck that there was absolutely no time for adjustment—none at all—and so was Leon. He had never worked with contact cement before either even though he was a handy guy and had been around. I've used the stuff since on many projects, but I'll always recall the kitchen cabinet at Split Rock and how unforgiving contact cement is.

CUTTING DOWN THE SPRUCE TREE
Fall 1967

In THE FALL OF 1967, when the tourist season was slowing down to a trickle of visitors, Leon had an idea that we should cut down the big spruce that was close to the lighthouse tower. As visitors came to the lighthouse, they came from the west and walked toward the east, past the residences. As they turned the corner, the lighthouse came into view, and they started to take pictures from there. Between the visitors and the lighthouse was a huge spruce tree about thirty to forty feet high that was very full at the base. Its branches blocked the view, and many people complained they couldn't get a snapshot from that location because the tree was in the way.

After numerous complaints Leon said that it had to go. When it did, so would the complaints of the picture-taking public. The details of the tree removal are rather dim, however Leon was a resourceful guy who borrowed a chainsaw and rope from some other Coast Guard station, probably Two Harbors.

We tied the rope in the high part of the tree and hooked the other end to the jeep to stop the tree from falling onto the chain link fence that surrounded the houses. Len used the chain saw, and I was in the jeep to keep tension on the tree. The spruce came down with a resounding crash right where we hoped it would fall, and we delimbed it and cut it in to small chunks so we could haul it away. Between the western most house (our house) and the winch house, just past the edge of the lawn and in amongst the rock, was the Split Rock dump. We didn't have garbage pick up in those days, so we just threw the trash into the dump and burned what was combustible. Therefore, even though it was a lot of material, we loaded the chunks of the tree and branches into the trailer and hauled it over to the Split Rock dump.

The evergreen tree that Leon and Mike cut down after many visitors complaints that the tree obstructed their view as they wanted to take a picture of the lighthouse when they came around the corner of the fence near the first house. (Photo Doris Woodard)

BIG STORM
Winter 1967-1968

IN THE EARLY WINTER OF 1967, a terrific northeastern storm hit the lake and the lighthouse. The wind blew until I thought the houses would blow away. It knocked out all the electricity, and the Kohler generator up in the lighthouse office took over and kept the light shining throughout the night. Leon and I stayed up to make sure the beacon was doing the job and on time. The wind was blowing the spray over the cliff from the east. When the spray from the lake hit the trees, it froze and created huge icicles. Some of the brush and branches of the birch trees snapped under the weight of the ice. The cement stairs and railings going up to the lighthouse tower were coated with ice and treacherous; we had to hang on for dear life.

The Kohler light plant did an excellent job, just as it was designed to do, and kept the 1,000,000 candle powered light signal on so as to provide a visual guide to any poor mariner unlucky lucky enough to be out on the lake in early December. A few years later, the *Edmund Fitzgerald* went down in a storm just like the one we experienced that night. The morning after, the sun came out, the birch trees and brush along the rim of the east cliff and out on the lawn was covered with a crystal sheeting of ice. With the morning sun shining through the ice on the trees, it was a spectacular sight.

I walked the trail to the old pump house down below the hill near the shore. At the bottom, the trees and branches were covered by ice. They groaned and tinkled as they were blown by the wind. The light shining through the trees and branches looked like jewels as they shimmered in the early morning sun.

THE ARTIST WHO WAS A THIEF
Winter 1967-1968

THERE WERE A FEW BIG STORMS on the lake when I was stationed there. After one such storm out of the northeast, I took some slides from below the lighthouse near the old pump house. I remembered how beautiful it was after the storms. I snapped many good shots in the early morning just after the sun was up. I didn't take too many pictures as we couldn't afford to have them developed into pictures or slides. We had the roll of film developed in the drug store in Silver Bay, and they were spectacular. I caught all the winter scenes, and the light was just right.

Later that winter, an artist from Chicago knocked on our door and asked permission to go through the property to get to the pump house scenery down below.

He didn't need permission as it wasn't a restricted area; he just wanted to do it right. After a short conversation, I said that I wasn't doing anything special and I'd go with him to lead the way. He didn't have the type of clothes needed for tramping around in the woods and snow, so we lent him some warm clothes and high boots. We walked through the deep snow to the bottom where he took lots of great pictures and said he was going to paint some landscapes from those photos.

We trudged back up the hill to the house, and he thanked us profusely for my time and attention and warm clothes. Before he left, he asked if we had taken any pictures of the lighthouse and surrounding area during or shortly after one of the big storms. We said yes we had, and he asked if he could see our photos. We proudly brought the slides out and he ooohed an aaaahed over them and said that they were just what he was trying to capture with his photos earlier that day. He then asked if he could maybe take some of our slides, make some copies, send them back to us and give us a little something for our troubles. Well, we were always short on money, and we didn't need the pictures for anything right then, and he said he would send them right back to us. As he said he'd send them right back after he made duplicated copies, Mary and I thought we'd let him have the slides. It would only take a couple of weeks or so. He again thanked us again, gave me his business card and left with our photographic treasures, the record of the aftermath of nature's fury. We never heard from the guy again. We never did figure it out if he was an out-and-out crook and a thief or just someone who came under the heading of "The road to hell is paved with good intentions." I misplaced his business card in one of our many moves over the years, so I can't remember his name or the name of his studio. I have never seen any of the pictures we gave him in either paintings or prints. This incident taught both Mary and me a life lesson that can only be learned the hard way. It had a profound effect in our trusting others throughout our lives and probably prevented us from being taken in or fooled by people over the many years since the lesson of the disappearing pictures at the Split Rock Lighthouse.

TV SHOW
Summer 1968

IN THE SUMMER OF 1968, a television crew came to Split Rock to do a video on the operation of the lighthouse. Bruce Robb was the officer in charge at the time. We showed the television crew around, and they shot a lot of video of the various parts of the lighthouse and the surrounding grounds. In one particular segment, they had us go up in the tower and through the man door and pretend to clean the glass windows of the light. They then had us sweep and clean off the catwalk around the top of the tower. Some close ups were taken from down near the paint shed, and the camera zoomed in on us sweeping and cleaning. All the video was completed in a couple of hours and was played on TV a week or so later on a weekly show that highlighted points of interest in northern Minnesota. It was fun to watch ourselves going about our daily tasks at the lighthouse even if some of them were staged. Split Rock and lighthouses in general have a special place in the hearts of many people, and they like to know as much as they can about them

THREE GUYS IN A CANOE
Summer 1968

DURING THE COURSE OF EACH DAY, we did many chores from turning the light on and off (our main job) to up dating the station log book and cleaning and polishing the lens of the light. On one such occasion, I was up on the light deck cleaning and polishing the lens, which looked like large prisms with a bull eye right in the middle. The brass that held the prisms of the lens needed polishing too. While taking a little break from that I happened to look toward the northeast out over the lake toward Canada. It was a sunny, crystal-clear day with no haze. I could see a small orange speck way off in the distance about ten to fifteen miles away. As I worked from time to time, my eyes would search for the orange speck out on the water. I wondered what the heck it was.

The view to the southwest from the base of the Split Rock lighthouse. (Photo Doris Woodard. Used with permission)

The orange speck was slowly coming closer and closer. After a long time and many visual checks, I could it was some type of a watercraft heading toward the lighthouse. This really piqued my interest, so I looked more often to get to the bottom of this orange mystery. We didn't have any fieldglasses on the station, and this would have been a good time to lobby for their procurement. The frequency of checking to see what it was, increased as the craft got closer and closer. Eventually I could make out three men wearing orange life preservers in a small nineteen-foot aluminum canoe. I was absolutely flabbergasted at their boldness . . . or was it stupidity? Lake Superior was not really the venue for small boats. It could be a cruel and dangerous lake.

As they paddled past the lighthouse, I leaned over the railing and yelled down at them, "Are you guy's nuts or what?" They said they didn't see what I was all excited about as the lake was perfectly clam. As they continued on, I thought of the old adage "God protects drunks and idiots" I didn't see any indication that they were drinking, so they had to be the latter category. I didn't read later about any search party looking for them in the paper, so they must not have drowned. Maybe to this day they still talk about the time they tweaked the nose of Mother Nature with their canoe ride on Lake Superior and she didn't kill them. I'm sure that I, as the nervous Coast Guardsman at the Split Rock lighthouse who yelled down at them and asked if they were nuts also might come up in the conversation as well. The lake is a huge cold body of water that can turn ferocious in about fifteen minutes. Take chances in a bathtub, not on Lake Superior. It is so cold that a person probably wouldn't drown if he went in but die of hypothermia. It instantly takes a person's breath away to hit that icy water and prospects of swimming to shore from an capsized canoe, even with shore in sight, would be slim to none.

Overturned from a boat, even with a life vest on, a person has just about enough time to kiss your fanny good-bye before the cold does its work. On one of our agate picking adventures on the Beaver River, which runs down from the hills into Beaver Bay on the lakeshore, I put one foot in the river, which was a brown color and the other one in the lake, which was clear. The foot in the lake felt like it was on fire, while the one from the River was warm. Fire, cold fire. That's how cold the lake is. After serving on search and rescue on the lake, I would never venture out on Lake Superior again for any reason. That lake scares the hell out of me.

MEMORABLE LIGHTHOUSE VISITORS
Summers of 1967 and 1968

DUE TO THE LARGE INFLUX OF SIGHTSEERS going through the lighthouse grounds all of whom seemed to want to talk, I would go into my garage and close the sliding door to work in peace during my off-duty time. I was building picnic tables for my stepfather in Ely. I got a lot of work done most of the time, but one night, the sliding door flew open, and a huge man stepped inside into the light. He said in a booming voice, "I was in the Navy, and I'll bet you can't guess what my rate was." I said that was easy, he was a boatswain's mate. He looked shocked and said I was right. He then asked how I liked the Coast Guard. I told him it was three square meals a day and home every night and weekend, and he agreed that it was good duty. He talked about his Navy experiences, how much he enjoyed them and how sometimes he wished he had reenlisted. After a while and a few stories later, he went to find his wife and kids who had walked on ahead.

Many wonderful people came to Split Rock, and a few come to mind. A couple from Finland came down from Thunder Bay and knocked on the lighthouse office door when I happened to be in there and asked for a middle-of-the-winter tour. I had a heck of a time understanding them as they had very thick accents, but they were overjoyed with the scenery and hospitality. They wanted to pay me they were so happy to see everything, but I declined their offer. Some biologists from Reserve Mining Company in Silver Bay climbed the tower to look for dark-colored water as a sign of pollution. A retired guy and his wife from Lombard, Illinois, tried to explain how to bring the shine back on our aluminum trailer. If I was up in the tower office and there

The entrance to the Split Rock Lighthouse and grounds looking northwest from our house. We closed the gate at sun down every night and before all inspections and opened them up again in the morning. (Photo Doris Woodard. Used with permission)

weren't any people around due to the season, time of day or the weather, I would sometimes give a tour but most of the time not.

One summer day, while I was painting the top of the pillars at the gate entrance
to the lighthouse, a young man and his folks walked by and said hi. The guy looked
familiar, but I just couldn't place him. When they came back, I asked him if I knew
him from somewhere. He said I looked familiar too. After a short conversation, we
found that the common denominator was Coast Guard boot camp in Cape May, New
Jersey. He had been there at the same time as I was. We had both seen one another
there but had actually never met. He was stationed in Chicago. Small world.

WORKING AT THE HOLIDAY STATION, DRUNK SNOWMOBILERS IN TWO HARBORS
Fall & Winter 1968

IN THE FALL OF 1968, I applied for and got a job at the Holiday Gas station and
convenience store on the corner of Highway 61 and Lake County 2 in Two Harbors.
Christmas was coming, and we needed extra money to make it merry, so I went to
work on the midnight shift as the cashier, shelf stacker, and clean-up maintenance guy.
I think the actual title was store clerk. It was quite a comedown for an ex-journeyman
pipefitter and diesel mechanic apprentice, but money was money, and things at Split
Rock were pretty laid back except for snow removal, building up-keep, and security.

It was a truly interesting job as it had to do with people and anytime as person has
a people job, you never know what's going to happen. The main part of the job early in
the shift was cashier for all of the late-night customers going home from afternoon shift.
There were also people coming home from an evening's entertainment downtown or just
plain night owls who were out and about. Two such night owls were a couple of young
guys about nineteen or twenty on snowmobile who would stop by from time to time. As

I recall, one of the snowmobilers was related to the
Kendall Smoked Fish people down in Knife River and
was called up to go in the service soon. On one particularly cold night, they came into the store well after
midnight and had a gallon jug of wine they were passing back and forth. They even offered me a snort, but
I was working and couldn't partake. They weren't too
drunk yet, so they bought whatever they came in for
and, with a roar, went racing up the street toward the
hospital and out of town.

Holiday station store sign, circa
2009 (Photo Mike Roberts

An hour or so later, they came back, a lot drunker and one had blood running down the front of his snowmobile suit. He still seemed to be bleeding but feeling no pain. I asked what had happened, and he said he hit the top of the windshield on his snow machine and cut his lip. Cut his lip was an understatement or what? He had laid his lip open in his mustache area from one side of his smile line to the other about an inch and a half above his mouth. As he excitedly told me what had happened, the blood bubbles were frothing from his exhaled breath, and his lip was hanging down so I could see his teeth and gums inside his mouth through the cut opening. They had come in from the dark night and probably didn't know how bad a cut it was. I'm not a medical guy, but I'd bet it would take at least fifteen to twenty stitches to close it up.

Being pretty looped, they both didn't seem to grasp the severity of the injury. As they passed the wine jug to each other in the store, the guy with the cut would push his drooping lip up and take a swig from the jug. When he tipped the jug up to drink, the wine seeped out the cut and ran down the front of his snowmobile suit mixed with the blood. The blood and the wine were dripping on my clean floor. As how I was the clean-up guy, I talked his partner into taking him up to the hospital emergency room to have him stitched up. They left going north on Highway 2 toward the hospital. I'll bet he sobered up when the doctor fixed that mess up. Those two young men must have gone into the service shortly afterwards as I never saw either one of them again..

RED FRIKEN, THE COP AT THE HOLIDAY
Fall & Winter 1968

RED FRIKEN WAS A PATROLMAN for the City of Two Harbors Police Department. While many of the town cops stopped by at the Holiday station from time to time to shoot the breeze and break up the night shift, I remember Red more than any of the others. He was solidly built guy who knew that he was a solidly built guy and was a no nonsense kind of police officer. Congenial on the surface, underneath, when push came to shove, I wanted to have Red on my side. He carried a long black, four-celled flashlight that would double as a Billy club if needed, and there was no doubt he used it more than once in his line of work. As a great storyteller, Red ranked right up there with the best of them. I recall him telling me of a shoot-out he was involved in a few years earlier. From his description and enthusiasm for relating the story, it was probably the highlight of his police officer career. I believe that Red lived for the exciting part of his job, like most of the people in law enforcement, and that was pretty much why they did the job. Then again someone has to do it.

CLEAN AND WAX AT THE HOLIDAY
Fall & Winter 1968

As THE MIDNIGHT CLEAN-UP MAN at the Holiday, I started work at 11:00 P.M. and was finished at 7:00 A.M. If there was one thing that the military had taught me, it was how to clean and polish. I would wait until about 1:00 or 2:00 A.M. to start the clean up so there weren't too many convenience-store customers coming in. I'd sweep and damp mop up all the aisles and, after they dried, apply the liquid wax. Now came my favorite part of floor care. After the wax was dry, I'd take the circular, revolving floor buffer I borrowed from the Two Harbors Coast Guard Light Station and buffed those floors until they just shined. Side to side and down each aisle I went, being careful not to let the buffer get away from me and wreck the bottom shelf merchandise, which could easily happen. When I was done, the floors looked like I could eat off of them, not that I wanted to. I got a sense of personal satisfaction from knowing it was a job really well done. No else one noticed or cared how nice it looked, not even the boss, but I did take pride in those cleaned and polished floors.

I had a lot of time to fill at that job. It was sometimes boring just standing around waiting for customers in the middle of the night, and it made me sleepy, too. I only waxed the floors once a week, so that didn't take so much of my time. Sometimes it was tough coming home after being up all night at the Holiday station and then working around the lighthouse too. But we needed money for Christmas presents and working at Holiday was a good way to earn it.

Another cleaning project that I undertook at the Holiday was the bathrooms. Like most public restrooms, they were functional but kind of grimy and grungy. Both the men and women's bathroom were just as bad, but the floors were a total disaster with many spots of old, discolored wax build up. Many coats of wax had been applied but never removed. I applied the wax stripper and lifted away all of the old wax. After many applications, I finally got those floors to look like they should. After I put down the new wax, it was looking pretty good. Then came my favorite part, buffing. I again borrowed the commercial buffer from the Two Harbors Coast Guard station. I buffed those floors until even some of the customers commented on how great they looked. The pay wasn't too good, but I did get a great deal of personal satisfaction from taking a sow's ear and trying to make a silk purse out of it. The checks didn't bounce—another good thing—and we had a very merry Split Rock Lighthouse Christmas.

THE CAR FULL OF DRUNKS ON NEW YEARS
Winter 1968

I WAS WORKING AT THE HOLIDAY STATION STORE on New Years Eve when a 1960 Ford white station wagon pulled up to the gas pumps. The windows were frosted up all of the way around except for the driver's side windshield. It was really cold out— twenty to thirty below zero, but I thought it was strange for the entire window to be so frosted up on a newer car. It was a four door. All the doors opened, and people started piling out, it looked like a clown car from the circus, there were a lot of people getting out, they just kept coming. They even came out through the back tail gate. There must have been eight to ten guys in that station wagon.

As the guys from the car came in, I could tell that they had been at a party and feeling no pain—all seemed to be a bit looped. The driver came in to warm up as the car filled with gas. From his actions and speech, I could tell that he was drunk too. The driver keep saying in a deep down south accent, "My momma will never believe this."

I finally asked him, "Believe what?"

He said, "That I'm in northern Minnesota, where the temperature is thirty below zero with a car full of drunks on New Year's Eve." Probably not.

They all seemed pretty mellow even though they were plowed. As each one paid for their items from the convenience store, they moved to the side of the check out to warm up and let the next person pay up.

The driver was the last to pay—with the money he had collected from the guys standing around warming up. For the third or fourth time he told me that his mother would not still believe him. I asked him where his momma lived, and he said "Louisiana." I asked him where he was going, and he mumbled something about a pulp-cutting camp up in the woods near Forest Center. After he warmed up for a while, he herded everyone back into the station wagon and drove off, going north on Lake County Highway #2. I never read anything in the paper about the sheriff finding a car full of frozen people in the ditch back in the boonies on New Year's Eve so I assumed they made it to their destination.

A COUPLE FIGHTING IN THE STORE
Winter 1968

THE STATION WAGON FULL OF DRUNKS had just left the Holiday station when a husband and wife walked in. They didn't have a vehicle that I could see, as the parking lot and pumps were empty. They stopped in to buy some cigarettes, and both were really drunk. They fumbled around to find the money for smokes and, after paying, got into an argument at the check-out counter. He called her names, and she shouted worse ones at him, I thought they were going to start pounding on one another right there. Then, he stomped out the door leaving her behind, and she watched him go. We had a movable sign on a pole with a heavy base on the gas island with something like "Pull Forward to the last Pump" on it. As he stomped away from the store and walked toward the island, he ran right in to the sign and knocked it over, and then fell down on top of it. He lay there for a little while. The woman, seeing her partner fall down on the sign, ran out to help him up. After struggling to his feet, he grabbed her arm, and together they walked off into the minus-thirty-degree night, headed home I hoped.

As I reflect back on these happenings and customers' antics, I can't but wonder if they all made it someplace safe without freezing to death. I don't recall ever hearing anything about them, so, in the words of my Uncle Martin Christnagel, "No News Is Good News" A couple of days later, we got the news that the Split Rock Light Station had been decommissioned and would close soon. I quit the Holiday Station Store job soon after New Year's due to circumstances beyond my control.

I was given a good recommendation for another job with Holiday if I wanted to work for them again. I did work for Holiday part time in Grand Marais for a short time while stationed there, but it wasn't something I wanted as a career.

Burned Down garage at Split Rock
February 1969

THE WOODARDS WERE OUR NEXT DOOR NEIGHBORS at Split Rock for the first year or so. Then they were transferred to Bayfield and from there to Port Huron, Michigan, where Leon served on a mobile boarding team. They boarded boats and checked them for safety violations along Lake Huron and Lake St. Clair. They were replaced by a young couple—Bruce and Kathy Robb. Bruce was a second-class bosun's mate with less than four years in the service. His home of record was Des Plaines, Illinois. Kathy worked in Duluth, which was quite a long daily commute. They had no children, just a black poodle dog named PoCo. They were always on the go and were not happy at Split Rock as it was too far out in the boonies, and everything they wanted was always in the city. The Robbs mutualed with Jim and Carol Schubert, stationed at the Two Harbors Light Station. The Schubert's home of record was Mineral Point, Wisconsin, and they were excited about coming to Split Rock. Carol also worked in Duluth, but she cut back on her hours when they moved to the lighthouse.

Schuberts had just bought a new Dodge 440 car, and Jim wanted to wash it. The third garage was our work shop, and we had a two-pot oil burner in it for heat. We didn't heat the garage all of the time; we shut the heater off when we weren't working in it. How the oil burner worked was this: the oil would flow in to the bottom of the combustion chamber by gravity. I would turn it on, wait a couple of minutes for the oil to run into the bottom of the pot, and then throw a lighted, twisted piece of paper. It would ignite. The higher I turned the control, the more oil ran in and the hotter the stove got. The heater warmed the garage nicely, and I could work in my shirt sleeves after a while, as there was a fan on the heater that blew the heat around the shop.

There were a couple of drawbacks with the oil burner, though. When lighting the burner with twisted paper, I had to make sure the oil started right away. If it didn't I would have to light another piece of paper and toss it in to get it going. If it didn't start the burner up, I had a problem. The oil would still be running into the bottom of the pot. If the flame went out during the start up, I would have to shut of the control and sop up the oil from the bottom of the pot with an old rag to keep the stove from over heating when it did light. This was the idiosyncrasy of a pot type oil burner.

The other drawback of the oil stove in our work garage was the prevailing west wind at Split Rock, which would cause a down draft and blow out the oil stove before it got hot. I was raised in the north and had a lot of experience with oil burners and lots of respect for them as they were unpredictable when they are heating up. Once they are up to temperature, a person could hardly blow them out.

Leon Woodard and Bruce Robb, like me, followed the oil burner start up procedure taught by experience. Jim Schubert either didn't get it or blew off the cautionary instructions. I guess I never asked him what part was murky to him. It was way below zero and really cold the day Jim decided to wash his new set of wheels. He started the oil burner as usual, but instead of waiting around until the stove got up to heat, he went back in to his house where it was nice and warm and waited for the garage to heat up. He went back out and found that the garage was still cold as the heater had gone out. The oil, of course, had kept running in to the bottom of the pot and had not burned off. He didn't sop up the excess oil, however, but just lit a twisted piece of paper and again threw it in to the oil stove, closed the door and went back in to the house to wait for the garage to heat up.

The sound powered phone in my quarters rang, and I answered it. Jim frantically yelled, "The garage is on fire! Call the fire department!"

Each of us probably has a picture in our mind of what we would do in an emergency—be calm, cool and collected was my mind's eye picture of my behavior under immediate stress and danger. I promptly called the Silver Bay Police Department who wouldn't take my call, but said I had to call the Fire Department. (This was before 911.) I got a hold of the right department, and they said they would be right out. It took about half an hour for them to get there. After Jim called and I was talking to the authorities, I looked out the kitchen window and saw flames shooting out of the garage door windows. All the buildings were set pretty close together, so we didn't know if the houses were going to burn too, so I got Mary and Mark out of our house and into our car which we drove out in to the gift shop parking lot, far way from the flames. Carol, who was pregnant, joined Mary, who was also pregnant with Eric in the car as they wondered what was going to happen next.

The fire department finally showed up in about twenty-five minutes or so—it was a long way from Silver Bay—and, of course, it seemed like forever before they came. They brought a fire engine and a tanker truck full of water and sprayed water

The site of the third garage/wookshop burned to the ground on January 29, 1969. Note the burned car on the left and the paint shed on the right. (Photo Mike Roberts)

on the houses and pump house to keep them from catching fire. They tried to rescue the blazing garage, but it burned to the ground with Jim's brand new car inside. As the garage was burning, the car horn started to blow and sounded for a very long time before it finally quit. I have since seen other car fires, and the uncontrollable blowing of the horn is characteristic of that kind of disaster.

The garage had a steel-shingled roof, and the wind created by the fire carried the shingles high in the sky. I'll bet some of those steel shingles can still be found off in the woods around the lighthouse. After the fire, the Coast Guard held an investigation to the cause and results of the mishap, but I never did see or hear of their conclusions. Many years later, I asked Jim if he ever settled up with the Coast Guard on the loss of his car, and he said they never paid him a dime. Bummer. We now had the clean up responsibility. What a mess. Jim rented an oxy-acetylene torch from Beaver Bay, and we cut up the burned out hulk of his car in to manageable pieces and hauled them up to the Beaver Bay dump. The fire was so hot it melted the carburetor down into the intake manifold. Jim sold the engine, transmission, axles and other heavy pieces to the junk man. What an experience! We are supposed to learn something from the happenings in our lives and what I learned that day was a great respect and awe for the power and destructiveness of fire.

GARAGE SALE
January 1969

WE HELD A GARAGE SALE IN JANUARY during the middle of the coldest part of winter of 1969 after the closing of Split Rock was announced by Group Duluth. We didn't have very much to sell, but we wanted to get in on the news that all of the north shore was talking about Split Rock Lighthouse closing. Mary baked cookies and cupcakes and made some Kool-Aid, hot apple cider, and coffee. People came looking for lighthouse antiques, but they were disappointed when there were none for sale. I do recall selling an old Damascus double-barreled shotgun with side hammers that was made by the American Gun Company. I had bought it in Walt Breen's junk shop in Ely before I went into the service. I also sold my four-string tenor banjo that I had been dragging around for years but never did learn how to play. We sold some old books and records and miscellaneous stuff we should have gotten rid long ago. It was so cold that we just about froze to death waiting for customers. The cookies, cupcakes and Kool-Aid all froze as it was just too cold. Few people came, so the last garage sale at Split Rock was a flop.

BOARDING UP SPLIT ROCK
March 1969

AFTER SPLIT ROCK LIGHTHOUSE CLOSED for the season in the latter part of December 1968, we were notified on New Year's day of 1969 that the light station was going to be decommissioned and permanently closed. Both of our families, the Schuberts and us were absolutely shocked and saddened at the news. We were given a choice of where in Group Duluth we might want to go for our next duty station. The Schuberts chose the Search and Rescue Lifeboat Station in Bayfield, Wisconsin. Mary and I chose North Superior Lifeboat Station in Grand Marais, Minnesota, just up the shore.

Mike and Mary Gehm were stationed at Grand Marais. He and I had been stationed together in Duluth, and he said Grand Marais was a good place to be, so we thought it might be a good move for us to go there to finish my enlistment. I had about a year to go.

The United States Coast Guard didn't have any available housing for us to relocate into in Grand Marais, so we had to find our own quarters. After a futile search

The roadway, looking from the east toward the west between the garages and the houses. Note the burned out garage on the right across the way from the first house on the left. (Photo Jim Schubert. Used with permission)

The Split Rock houses and garages from the lighthouse tower looking northwest in the winter of 1969. (Photo Jim Schubert. Used with permission)

for an affordable apartment, we decided to buy a mobile home. When we found one, we could move it to the town of Grand Marais, and, after my enlistment was up, we could move it to Ely until we got the house there livable. Great plan. Now all we had to do was find a decent mobile home and move it to Grand Marais.

We looked but couldn't find one anywhere up the north shore. Then Mary spotted an ad for a 1955 ten-by-fifty Detroiter in Finland, Minnesota, so we went to look at it. It would do the job nicely as it had three bedrooms with a front living room and spacious kitchen. We dug it out of the snow in its parking spot in a trailer park close to the river and hired a drive-away company to move it up to Joe Thompson's Trailer Park on the east end of Grand Marais about a mile out on Highway 61. Mary was pregnant with our second child and was due any day. We borrowed against our life insurance policy to get the money to buy the trailer, and then sold a lake lot we had on the north shore of Fall Lake in Winton, Minnesota, to pay that money back.

I was an E-3 seaman and became a part of North Superior Lifeboat Station in Grand Marais as a boat crewman on search and rescue. I was also part of the team

Split Rock Lighthouse from the south side of the fog signal building in the winter of 1969. (Photo Jim Schubert. Used by permission)

chosen to board up the now closed Split Rock Lighthouse. I never did hear how we were chosen for the job as there were other stations closer. However, we were the boarding up team. We traveled to Split Rock daily with our tools and materials to get the job done. Members of the boarding-up crew were Chief Boatswain Mate Tom Whelan, Second-Class Engineman Jerry Galliard, Seaman Mike Gehm, Seaman Orrie Holmen, others I can't recall, and me, Seaman Mike Roberts.

With Mary so close to delivery, I was a little reluctant to go that far to do the job at Split Rock. The system of rank in the service leaves no doubt as to who is in charge, and the person in charge calls the shots. I had no choice but to go to Split Rock to help no matter what the circumstances. As luck would have it, Mary went into labor while I was gone on the boarding-up detail, so the officer in charge's wife, Lil Whalen, came and took care of Mark after she drove her to the hospital. When I got back to town at the end of a long day, Mary was almost ready to deliver. In today's day and age, I think they would have let me stay behind to tend to my family's needs, but that was then and this now, and times do change for the better. Our second son, Eric Louis Roberts, was born at 10:16 P.M. March 12, 1969, weighing six pounds nine ounces and was twenty inches long. He was a healthy baby boy.

Carol Schubert standing next to the third order Frensel lens in the light tower at Split Rock Lighthouse. Winter of 1969. (Photo Jim Schubert. Used with permission)

Boarding up Split Rock, our home for approximately twenty-six months was a difficult task. I liked the duty and the people at the lighthouse. It was a historical place and one that saved many lives during its long and colorful history. I felt as if the lighthouse was a part of me, and I was a part of the lighthouse. It had been our home. Little did we know when Mary and I went there in 1966 that we would be the last Coast Guard family to live there. I did not know nor could I have known that I would be the last Coast Guardsman of Split Rock Lighthouse.

Chapter Four

Chores and Duties of Split Rock

Cleaning the Light & Ready for Inspections
Summer 1967 & 1968

From time to time, we would get inspectors or dignitaries come to inspect the lighthouse, the grounds, and the dwellings. We always had advance notice that they were coming usually once or twice per year. We chipped, painted, mowed, pruned, weeded, cleaned, straightened, shined and polished everything that needed attention. The lighthouse was the show place of the station, and everyone wanted to see it at its best. The Kohler light plant was located on the right or north coming into the tower office. It was a four-cylinder gasoline engine painted gray with a generator connected to it. In the event of a power outage, the generator would replace the power company's electricity and provide power to the lighthouse. The outstanding feature of the light plant was the radiator with its brass top.

In the lighthouse office was a steel office desk with the station log book on it. A few other books, including a phone book, had their place on the desk, and, toward the back, sat the telephone. In front of the desk was a swivel chair on wheels that pushed into the desk when not in use. On the wall to the left of the desk was a chart that listed the times of the rising and setting sun. Centered over the desk was a window that faced the west. From the office a hallway to the left led to the lighthouse tower. Upon entering the tower base to the left a few paces was a gray circular stairway with a handrail that lead up to the light itself. The steel steps and steel painted handrail wound around and was connected to the inside of the wall which was a white brick or ceramic tile.

In the very center of the tower was a gray cylinder that rose from the floor to ceiling which housed the weights that turned the light before electricity was brought to the light station. The weights were suspended by a cable that hung down in the inside center of the cylinder and the top part of the cable was connected to a winch contained in a wood and glass box. A crank inserted into the winch box turned and would wind up the cable and bring the weights up to the top of the cylinder ready to have gravity pull them down and turn the light. This system was much like the weight system of a grandfather clock mechanism.

I was absolutely fascinated by the brass balls of the governor that controlled the speed of the rotation of the lens of the light. The lens rode in a big container of mercury that buoyed up the base of the lens as it turned effortlessly in the enclosed mercury bath

Containers of extra mercury were stored near the base on the equipment deck. A ladder rose from the floor of the deck up into the center of the lens which gave access to the light and light changer and was also used for cleaning the inside of the lens.

Each part of the lens of the double-sided clam-shaped frensel light was separate and had a lengthwise rounded triangular shape, which concentrated the light into the center or bullseye of the lens itself. Each lens prism had to be cleaned with a glass cleaner of vinegar and water. The brass that surrounded the prism and held it in place was cleaned with a brass polish.

As I recall, the brass cleaner was a polish contained in a cotton batten type material, which was wiped on the brass, left to stand until it got a hazy film on it and then wiped off with a clean rag. We cleaned the brass first and then cleaned the glass of the lens. It took hours and hours of cleaning tedium to make the glass and brass clean and shiny enough to be ready for inspection. We washed and cleaned the huge windows surrounding the light facing the lake from time to time.

The back or landside of the light was shielded by rounded steel plates the same size as the glass. The plates were painted black, but I don't recall ever painting them during my service there. On the back of the tower, in the steel plates on the light deck to the northwest, was a man door that opened to allow cleaning of the glass windows from the outside. Anytime you opened that door, it was always windy, sometime it seemed as though you would be blown off the catwalk over the railing that surrounded the tower. We held on tight, it was a long way down.

We could see a little bit of the light shining out into the lake from the south side windows of our house. It gave us a feeling of comfort and wellbeing during our residence at Split Rock lighthouse

SPLIT ROCK DAILY CHORES, PLOWING
Winter 1967 & 1968

WE HAD A CJ5 JEEP THAT WE USED FOR TRANSPORTATION but mostly to plow snow around the station and out to the main road. When used for transportation, it wasn't the best vehicle to ride in. It had a short wheel base, so it was very rough riding. The springs and the rest of suspension were stiff, and the seats not too thickly padded either. After all it was a military Jeep. But it did the job, just not in comfort. It had four-wheel drive, though, which was needed during the winter plowing season. It had an enclosed cab with windows on the side, a good heater and snow plow on the front with an electric lift.

The lift was a hydraulic jack that had a cap over the spring loaded pumping rod. The spring brought the rod to the UP position so it could be pumped down again.

The Coast Guard Split Rock Light Station CJ5 Jeep. (Photo Doris Woodard. Used with permission)

A twelve-volt electric starter motor supplied the circular motion. On the end of the starter motor was a cam, which, when turned, would push the rod down and raise the plow up. A lever in the cab operated the device that let the plow drop. The only draw-back of this ingenious store-bought labor-saver was if the plow was lifted up with the starter motor too many times in a row, it would drain the battery. That still wasn't too bad because the generator could keep up, but if you killed the Jeep's engine, when plowing too vigorously into a snow bank and the battery, depleted by repeated lifting of the plow, didn't have the juice to start the Jeep anymore. That ended the plowing for the day until the battery could be recharged. Not a problem if I was close to a source of electricity. All I had to do was run the extension cord over to the dead Jeep, hook up the battery charger and plug it in. When the battery was charged up, I was ready to go.

However, if I was too far way from the station, and the cord wasn't long enough to reach, I'd have to take the battery out and bring it back to the shop to recharge it or get my car and jump the Jeep to get it started, and then bring it back to the shop garage to charge it up overnight.

The snow plow was painted yellow and was made by the Meyers Company. It had adjustable feet on the bottom so you wouldn't wear out the cutting edge. The plow was mounted so it could swivel either straight, left or right. It had a strong spring so it you hooked or hit something with the blade it wouldn't break the undercarriage of the Jeep but the plow tipped forward and then sprung back in position after the tension was taken off from it. A plow saving idea to be sure.

During the winters of 1967 and 1968, there was plenty of snow. At times it seemed like it snowed all the time. I didn't mind as I loved to plow snow. Plow, not shovel. We plowed the road out to Highway 61 and kept it open all winter. Toward spring, the snow banks got closer and closer together because we could only throw the snow so far into the ditch with a Jeep-mounted snow plow. The county came in to save the day with their big snow plow truck with a wing plow out the side. They winged out the road, and we again had a place to put the snow.

The station also had that Jari mower with a sickle bar, and it had a snow blower attachment. The mower and snow blower could be swapped out to whatever job needed to be done. We mounted the snow blower on it at the end of October and left it on until May. Winter was a long season at Split Rock. The Jari did an excellent snow re-movable job, but in many places, such as at the light tower, it was too heavy to get up there, so we just shoveled the snow out of the pathways. When the shop garage burned to the ground in the winter of 1969, it burned the Jari up too. What a shame. It was a wonderful labor-saving machine.

PAINTING THE LH RING
Summer 1967

DURING THE FIRST SUMMER that I was stationed at Split Rock, Leon thought that the white ring surrounding the light tower below the top set of windows looked a little shabby

The Split Rock Lighthouse taken from the south side of the fog signal building. (Photo Doris Woodard. Used with permission)

and should be painted. As the station seaman and the lowest ranking member of a two-man team, the task was mine. The paint shed was the cement building to the east of the quarters and the garages, next to the gasoline pump and to the northeast of the light tower and fog signal building. After getting the paint out of the shed, mixing and stirring it up, I choose a four-inch brush to do the job. We had a twenty-foot wood extension ladder that extended out to approximately forty feet. Len and I put this ladder up against the side of the light tower and extended it up to the white ring. The old paint was peeling, so I scraped it off and very carefully started to apply the first coat of white paint.

It seemed like it was always windy up on the ladder way up there. Being on the ladder was safe enough as it was sturdy, but it had just a little sway as I climbed up and down. There was no way to tie the top off to keep the ladder from shifting, but I guess that's just the way it was. It didn't bother me too much as I had painted high aids to navigation structures when I was stationed in Duluth. However, when I looked out behind, out toward the lake and down at the rocks, it made me want to get a little closer to the ladder. It was a long way down. If the ladder shifted, I was a goner. It made me real happy when we moved the ladder around to the flat ground on the east side, near the fog signal building.

I don't remember painting the ring on the north side of the tower over the watch office roof. It must not have been too scary compared to the lake side of the light tower. The visitors all said that I had to be crazy to paint up in the air so high, but it was just part of the job at the lighthouse. I didn't look forward to painting the very top of the lighthouse tower. It was made out of metal and would have to be painted with an alkyd gloss red. As luck would have it, Woodard didn't see the need to paint the very top while he was there, and the lighthouse closed before it needed painting again, which didn't make me mad at all.

SCRAPING WHITE PAINT OFF THE STAIRS IN OUR QUARTERS
Winter 1967

THE QUARTERS AT SPLIT ROCK were comfortable and well kept. The tenants who occupied the house before us did a good job of keeping it up. What else did we have to do in the long winter but keep the houses in good shape? There were many, many coats of paint on the walls. If we didn't like the color, we could just paint them again. The Coast Guard supplied the paint at no cost to us. As I recall, our living room was a ghastly orangeish tomato soup color, and we really questioned the taste of the previous occupant/painter. Most of the woodwork throughout the house was painted white. Both houses on the property were built exactly the same with a stairway going up from the ground floor up to the second story in the same place in the house.

It was on the east side of the house going up the east wall. Some one from years past had painted the stairways in both houses white. Beneath the paint was a beautiful oak wood. Leon made the discovery and started to scrape away the white paint to get down to the oak wood below. He thought it would be a great winter project for each of us to scrape the stairway in our house. I never actually volunteered to scrape the stairway, but he implied than I should add it to my domestic to-do list. I really didn't have too much to do during the winter except make home-brew beer, sausages, polish agates and keep warm as I plowed snow and shoveled the sidewalks around the station. I conceded that it might be a good idea to refinish the stairs and it would look nice after it was finished. What a job! He scraped, I scraped, we scraped and scraped. Then we compared notes as to how the job was coming along. When it was finally done, it looked nice but, at that point, who cared. Little did we know at the time that they would close Split Rock Lighthouse within a year anyway.

SPLIT ROCK DAILY CHORES, TURNING THE LIGHT ON AND OFF
Winter 1968/1969

THE MAIN REASON THAT SPLIT ROCK existed was to warn lake farers of the danger associated with that part of Lake Superior. The lighthouse could be seen in the day time for approximately fifteen to twenty miles or further depending on the weather conditions. At night the visibility was about thirty miles, again depending on the conditions. It was a ten-second light which meant that it flashed every ten seconds. If a person timed the interval between flashes, a clear identification of the source being Split Rock could be made. It was a white light, a further characteristic of Split Rock. Not all lighthouses have white lights. Across the lake in the Apostle Islands, the Devils Island light is red, and I don't know how many other colors there are. Clearly, the point is that the interval and the color of the light could give ships a location, could let them know exactly which part of Lake Superior—and its shoreline—they neared.

The station personnel would turn the light on one half an hour before sun down and turn it off one half an hour after sun rise. It was our main job at the lighthouse and while I was stationed there, we never ever missed turning it off or on. Turning it on was much more important than turning it off. If it ran all day, it just cost the electricity the run it, but if you didn't turn it on at night, they would not be able find their location and be in danger.

The rest of the time we worked around the station, cleaning, painting, mowing and plowing depending on the season.

LIBERTY CARDS
Spring 1968

WHEN STATIONED AT A COAST GUARD STATION, the lower-ranking personnel were issued liberty cards or passes. Whenever they were away from their base, the sailors had to show some documentation upon demand by the authorities that they were not absent without leave or AWOL. During Woodard's tenure at Split Rock, we never discussed a liberty card, and I wasn't aware that I needed one on such a small station. When Robb transferred to Split Rock, he wanted to make sure that even if it was an isolated station, he followed procedures. Robb issued me a liberty card to cover my coming and going, just in case I ever got stopped for whatever reason. I would be in the clear as far as regulations go. It was most appreciated, but I never had the occasion to use it. Most of the time, we didn't go very far from Split Rock, just to Duluth to pick up groceries and occasionally to Ely to see my family. When going to Detroit to visit Mary's folks, we always took a leave as we each got thirty days of leave per year.

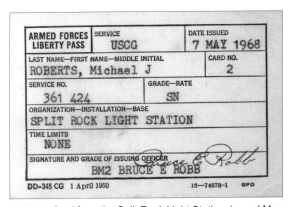

A Liberty Card from the Split Rock Light Station, issued May 7, 1968, and signed by Second-Class BM Bruce Robb. (Artifact Mike Roberts)

CHAPTER FIVE

FRIENDS AND FAMILY AT SPLIT ROCK

THE DAY MARK WAS BORN
September 8, 1967

MARY AND I BABYSAT THE WOODARD KIDS from time to time, more Mary than me. In September of 1967, the Woodards had gone to a Coast Guard party at the Superior Entry Light Station. I don't recall the occasion, but sometimes they didn't need an occasion, they just went visiting to see old friends. They had been in Group Duluth for a quite a while and had made a lot of friends.

Mary wasn't feeling too well that day as she was getting close to delivery. She was showing signs of labor starting and went up to the lighthouse to call the doctor. He told her to come to the hospital in Two Harbors to get checked because she was having contractions. The baby wasn't due for another month, so we thought she was having false labor. Split Rock is a long way from the Two Harbors hospital, and that was before they drilled a hole in Silver Cliff and ran the road through it. We definitely wanted the benefit of a doctor and hospital for the birth of our first child. Mary was "nesting" in preparation of the birth but did not know it at the time.

I called Superior Entry and told Leon and Doris that we were going to the hospital, and they should meet us there to pick up their kids. When we arrived, Mary, the kids, and I went in and Mary was hustled off for examination. The nurse said it looked like the birth was progressing right on schedule, so I kept an eye on the kids until their mom and dad picked them up. Mary's labor lasted until 12:47 A.M. when Mark arrived on the earthly scene. After mother and baby were resting, I called Mary's mom at about 2:00 A.M. and said, "Hello, Grandma?" She said, "I'm not a grandma," and I said, "You are one now." Grandma Mary Fodor then woke up the whole house right in the middle of the night to share the good news.

MARK CAME HOME FROM THE HOSPITAL
September 11, 1967

OUR SON MARK WAS BORN ON SEPTEMBER 8, 1967 in Two Harbors while we were stationed at Split Rock. He was just a little guy at birth, who was four weeks early,

weighed five pounds, six and one-quarter ounces and was so tiny he looked like a little bird. After Mary's hospital recovery, they said she and baby were ready to go home. I drove the 1961 red Pontiac station wagon up to the hospital door where they brought the new mom and baby out in a wheel chair. Mary climbed into the front passenger's seat, they handed her Mark, closed the door, backed up, wished us well and waved good-bye while we drove away. Holy Cow! What are we going to do now? Mary had a younger brother, Steve around when she was a teenager but that was our total baby experience. Now we have a baby of our own with no one to help or guide us and we were living way out in the sticks with the nearest doctor up in Silver Bay.

Our son Mark, one week old, taken on September 16, 1967, at our Split Rock home. (Photo Mike Roberts)

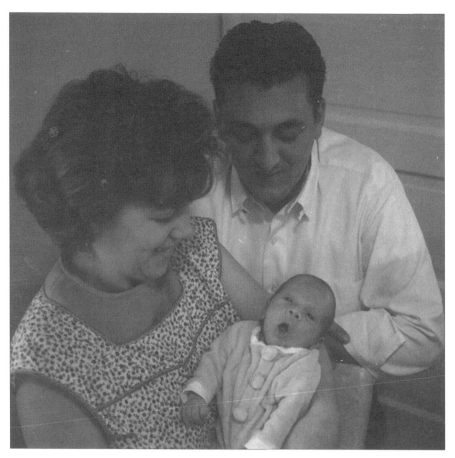

Mary holds Mark while Mike watches. Photo taken at our Split Rock home after Mark's baptism on October 1, 1967. (Photo Mary Roberts)

We were scared to death that we might do something wrong. We watched Mark like two hawks, afraid that he might choke or stop breathing and then what would we do? Well, babies are pretty tough and great communicators and they don't suffer in silence. When they are hungry, they cry. When they are wet, they cry. When they have gas, they cry. Then, just because its 3:00 A.M. on a Tuesday morning, they cry, for no apparent reason. After a time of bewilderment, sheer exhaustion and occasional panic, we got a book on raising babies by Dr. Benjamin Spock and that helped tremendously. We found that babies were for the most part pretty contented if they were feed regularly, kept dry and got plenty of sleep.

Our new baby took off and started to grow, gained weight, was happy and had a great personality. He also became a daddy's boy. I was around most of the time and spend a lot of time with him to the point that if I went into the bathroom, he would put his fingers under the door and cry, wanting to come in and join me. This lasted until we left Split Rock and went to Grand Marais. I was gone a lot of the time on Coast Guard duty and he finally got over it.

Mark, Our Baby at Split Rock
1967 & 1968

Mark was born on September 8, 1967, in Two Harbors and was baptized at St. Mary's Catholic Church in Silver Bay on October 1, 1967, by Father Golobich. My sister Shelia and her husband, Rusty, stood up as his godparents

He grew rapidly as he was so small at birth, 5 pound and 6 ¼ ounces. He was a happy and healthy child and we had lots of time to spend with him. He loved to have Winnie the Pooh read to him as he pointed to the illustrated pictures in the book.

As we lived at Split Rock, which was an isolated station, we didn't have many close people around. Mary and I were the only people at his first birthday party but we had a lot of fun playing games and eating cake and ice cream.

Mike reading a Winnie the Pooh book to Mark in our Split Rock living room. (Photo Mary Roberts)

He also liked to take baths on the kitchen table, didn't mind getting his hair washed and would laugh when the rinse water was poured over his head.

As he grew and he became more active, he had endless energy and was a daddy's boy. It was a special segment of our lives as we had the time to spend with our first born son. I considered myself most fortunate as I had the opportunity to help raise him. I lived where I worked, didn't have a long commute or need to spend large blocks of time earning a wage. Split Rock

Mark at six months, March 1968. (Mike Roberts collection)

Lighthouse was my job and my home.

CHRISTMAS
1966

MARY AND I SPENT THREE CHRISTMASES at Split Rock, between 1966 and 1968. They were happy times. At the Christmas of 1966, we were just happy to be together every

Mike, Mary, and Mark in their Split Rock home dining room. December 29, 1967. (Photo Mary Roberts)

71

night and every weekend. What a change from the duty in Duluth. We cut a tree from the nearby woods, dragged it home and put it up in the southwest corner of the dining room. We were married in 1964, so we had gathered some Christmas tree lights and decorations in our travels, and now we brought them out and put them on the tree. We gave each other simple and inexpensive gifts. The Woodards had gone home to North Carolina for the holidays, so we had the lighthouse all to ourselves. It was a bit lonely on the north shore as our neighbors were gone, and we didn't have any family close, but it was a happy time too. We had each other to share the Christmas season of 1966 with.

MAKING CHRISTMAS PRESENTS
1968

WHEN WE WERE STATIONED AT SPLIT ROCK, we never made very much money as was mentioned earlier. Every day was an economic struggle just to pay the bills and keep our household going. In our families, it was traditional to give everyone gifts at Christmas time. Mary and I thought long and hard as to how we were going to keep the family giving tradition alive. Mary came up with the idea, instead of buying people gifts as was past practice, we would make all of their Christmas presents while we were at Split Rock.

I had a bunch of leather working tools, given to me by someone, so purses, wallets, and checkbook covers were going to be part of the gifts to family. In order to make these items, I needed leather. On one of our trips to Duluth, we stopped at the Tandy Leather Shop on Superior Street and bargained with them, trying to get their wares as economically as possible. There was also a leather luggage maker down town where I stopped and asked if I could buy some of their leather scraps. I explained that I was in the service and stationed at Split Rock and we were making all of our Christmas gifts out of leather this year. They were very kind and understanding, giving me lots of their scraps, which I suspect weren't scraps at all but good leather.

When it came to stamping the designs on the leather, I had to hit the leather design tool with a hammer. Every time I would hammer the tool, it would make a loud noise, and Mark would jump in his sleep but it wasn't enough to wake him up. I guess he just got used to the racket associated with making leather goods in time for the Christmas of 1968.

We worked for a couple of months or so making the gifts in anticipation of the Christmas holiday. We made many bottles of balloon wine and sealed them in molten wax. I had a wood lathe down in our basement, so I turned out salad bowls big and small and made a few lamps too. We scrounged for more wood. My stepdad, Bill Wegner, had lots of it and was more than generous. He even found some black walnut and birch, which I promptly made into butcher block cutting boards. We gave one to my sister, Shelia, and I made one for Mary. We used that board for about thirty years, but it finally started to delaminate so was tossed out.

Mary sewed full aprons for her mom and grandmother, Christmas stockings for my sister Shelia's kids, filled with tasty goodies, with their names on them. She even sewed three stockings for us. She had a lot of practice and was getting pretty good on the sewing machine, so she made herself some maternity clothes, as we were expecting our second child in March. We also made many different kinds of fudge. Mary baked Spritz and Christmas cookies galore. She even made *Kiflee*, a Hungarian walnut filled pastry handed down in her family for generations. We were very happy creating the Christmas treasures for family, as we had lots of time to be creative and enjoyed sharing our talents with everyone.

Mark was fifteen months old at the Christmas of 1968 and was aware that it was a special time. He liked the Christmas tree, especially the hanging ornaments and tinsel. If we didn't watch him closely, he would chew on the ones shaped like green balls. When he got his gifts, he tore the wrapping paper off after we showed him how to do it. He played with all of his presents, but he liked the pots, pans, and lids the best. He banged them together with great abandon.

We hand delivered the Ely gifts to my family and the post office took our box full of treasures to Detroit. From time to time, Mary and I still laugh about our lack of money at Split Rock, which wasn't very funny at the time, and how much fun we had making all of the gifts for everyone, trying to make due with very little. It builds character.

PAINTING DISNEY CHARACTERS AT SPLIT ROCK
Late Fall 1967

WHEN MARY AND I WERE EXPECTING Mark in the summer of 1967, we had no idea what to expect, so we started to get the house ready for our first born. We decided that the bedroom in the northeast corner of the upstairs of our home would be the baby's room., Mary sewed curtains for the windows and I thought a Disney mural would look nice on the south wall. I was not a good artist, and in no way could I ever draw a mural that would remotely resemble any of the Disney characters, but we looked in books and magazines for inspiration and finally found some that I could trace with carbon paper. Now the problem was how enlarge and put them on the wall?

I took the frame of a blank slide and inserted the small Disney tracings that were done on paper. I put vegetable oil on the tracings to make them transparent and put the slide in the slide projector. When focused on the wall, the faint outline of Mickey and Minnie were visible. I moved the projector forward and back to get the right height and size, and then traced the outlines on the wall in pencil. I painted the inside of the lines the appropriate colors. When completed I had a fair redition of Mickey, Minnie Mouse, and Donald Duck happily smiling down on our precious newborn child. As Mark got older, he would stand in his crib and touch the paintings.

People who lived at Split Rock in later times informed me that the paintings were covered over by the new tenants during a redecorating phase of our old home.

FODOR'S BIG MEAL AT SPLIT ROCK
Summer 1968

AFTER MARY AND I WERE MARRIED in the summer of 1964 and left Detroit for Ely, Minnesota, in the spring of 1965, we didn't get much of a chance to spend time with her family. They were a close-knit, huggy, kissy bunch who was very family ori-

Pat Fodor climbing on the rocks below the cliff at Split Rock. (Photo Mike Roberts)

ented. When Mary's parents, Mary and Louie, came to visit us at Split Rock, along with the kids, in the summer of 1968, they were so happy to be with us, and we were happy that they came to Minnesota to see us. They stayed for a about a week. The day before they had to leave as their vacation was drawing to a close, Mary went all out and put on a meal fit for royalty. As the main course, she made her dad's favorite food, Hungarian stuffed cabbage with hot homemade rye bread, cookies, and a couple of fresh-picked blueberry and raspberry pies topped with ice cream.

After supper, we went for a walk down the trail to the bottom of the hill by the old pump house where Louie took a lot of pictures of the lighthouse on top of the high cliff. When he got them developed, they were his pride and joy. He showed them to all the relatives and neighbors back home as he explained that his daughter, Mary, lived at the Split Rock Lighthouse and had baked him pies. After our trip down the trail, we returned home, sat around the living room and stayed up late, talking about the day's happenings and all that Mary and Louie had seen on their North Shore vacation. After her parents went to bed, Mary, Pat, Steve, and I stayed up longer, talking and laughing until Louie hollered down the stairs that he had to drive home the next morning and wanted to get some sleep.

By early morning, they were packed up and ready to hit the road. Louie said that he had to take one last look at his grandson, Mark, who was taking a nap in the bedroom. He went upstairs to say good-bye to our sleeping baby. When he came down and was ready to leave for home, he said to Mary, "The next time I see you, honey, you'll have two little ones." He never got the chance to see our second child, Eric, who was born on March 12, 1969 in Grand Marais. Louie Fodor died of a heart attack on July 9, 1969, at the age of fifty-three in Detroit, one week before they were going to come to see us on their next Minnesota vacation.

GOING TO ELY ON HIGHWAY #1
Summer 1968

WHEN THE FODORS CAME TO SPLIT ROCK on vacation, one of the things we did was to take State Highway #1 up to Ely. Mary and Louie had visited us in Ely when we first moved back in 1965. During their 1965 trip, they met my mother, Helen Christnagel Roberts Wegner, and my stepfather Clarence "Bill" Wegner. The two grandmas and grandpas got along famously and genuinely liked one another. When Mary and Louie wanted to go and see them, we thought it was a wonderful idea. Usually I drove with the station wagon as there was more room, but this time Louie said he would like to drive. He had a 1956 Chevy Bel Aire sedan in real good shape. I rode shotgun. Steve sat in the middle, and Mary and Grandma Mary sat with Mark and Pat in the back.

State Highway #1 going from the North Shore to Ely is a scenic twisty-turny slow-driving road through the Superior National Forest. The deer, moose, and other woodland creatures are just waiting to jump in front of cars to test drivers' reflexes. Many vehicles have hit moose, deer, and bear along this intrusion into nature. In the summer of 1962 as we were returning home from a day at the North Shore picking agates, my folks and I had a deer jump right into the grille and hood of a brand new 1962 Chevy station wagon and wreck it.

I didn't want to tell Louie how to drive as he had been driving longer that I had been alive. However, I didn't want us to make the 6:00 TV o'clock news as casualties of a moose-and-car-crash either. So I told him ever so gently that this was a hazardous road and the faster he went the higher the probability of having a crash with a moose or deer. He, however, did not take the good driving tip and drove the road at the max-imum speed. On every curve, he mistook the sign that said thirty or forty miles per hour and thought that was the minimum speed to travel. Mary, Mark, and I hung on for dear life, full well knowing that this might be our last trip together. We were pet-rified. The rest of the family, oblivious to the ever-present doom and danger, was chatty and happy without a care in the world. We made it to Ely without mishap and had a great time visiting my folks.

About halfway back to the North Shore on the return trip, I couldn't stand the suspense anymore. In my nicest, non-confrontational voice, I asked Louie to please slow down before he killed us all. The message was well taken, and he backed off of the gas pedal for a little while. While driving in Detroit and the big city, there are ob-vious road hazards well recognized by all city drivers, but out in the sticks of northern Minnesota, the dangers do not stand out quite as blatantly. Louie didn't pick up on these dangers, and I wasn't forceful enough in my driving advice. We went careening around corners way too fast and sped down the straight stretches. When we finally got back to Split Rock, Mary and I were happy just to be alive. Anytime after that hair-raising trip down Highway #1, if we were going to go someplace with Mary's folks, I tried to drive whenever possible.

MARY, LOUIE, AND THE BEARS
Summer 1968

Mary's parents, Mary and Louie Fodor, her brother Steve and sister Pat lived in Melvindale, Michigan, a suburb of Detroit, and Louie worked in the Chrysler Auto Plant in Trenton. The highlight of their year was going on vacation, and as we had plenty of room at our house at Split Rock, they came to visit us. We were very excited to see them as we hadn't seen them since the early spring. Our Mark was their only grandchild. We did many things during their visit including sightseeing at Gooseberry Falls and picking agates along Flood Bay and the Split Rock River beaches of the North Shore.

At one point while they were with us, I asked the Fodor family if they wanted to see the bears. They said, "Bears, what bears?" Mary's mother was very protective of all of her children especially Steve, her youngest. He was Louie's constant companion,

Posing for a family picture while on a hike to the bottom of the Split Rock cliff. Left to right: back row: Pat Fodor, Mary Fodor, Louis Fodor; bottom row: Mike Roberts holding Mark, and Steve Fodor. (Photo Mary Roberts)

and they kept a close eye on his comings and goings. They wanted to make sure he never got in harm's way. So when I said, "Bears," they were curious but cautious. Up near Lax Lake was a dump where all of the local trash was brought by everyone for miles around. It was just thrown on the ground in a remote spot as was the custom in the 1960s. There was a chicken egg farm close by, and they too used the dump to dispose of their old eggs. Cracked and broken eggs and ones that had been candled out for having blood spots were deposited there, as well as other types of refuse from their egg operation. The dump was a bear magnet with plenty of delicious bear snacks especially the smelly old discarded eggs.

Bears are nocturnal and would come to the dump at twilight. What better way to see Mother Nature's scavengers than at the dump? We drove in about half an hour before dark, parked and waited for the bears show to begin. During the wait, Louie held his grandson, Mark, and made all of the grandfather noises to keep the baby interested and happy. Grandma Mary was watching Louie and baby communicate, but she kept her protective eyes peeled for the bears. The window on the Pontiac station wagon was getting a little steamed up as they were closed to keep the bugs and bears out. After sitting there for a while, Grandma Mary was getting a little antsy and said, "I don't see any bears. Maybe they won't come out tonight." Just about then, a huge black bear walked up from the front of the car, paused, then strolled past the passenger side window in search of food. Many others followed his lead and started coming out of the woods all around us. We watched them feed for a quite a while as they ripped things apart with their claws and teeth looking for tidbits.

Grandma Mary wasn't comfortable in the car surrounded by foraging bears. She exclaimed, "My God, they're every where" As it got darker, it got more difficult to see the bears, so, after a while, when it was almost pitch black, we decided it was time to go. As we left the dump, the headlight shone on the eyes and bodies of the creatures who came to feed and had provided the Fodor family with one of the highlights of their Split Rock Lighthouse vacation.

MARK'S CHILDHOOD MISHAP
Summer 1968

Mary was baking in the kitchen, and Mark was sitting on a chair drinking water from a hard plastic glass. Somehow, he fell off, landed on the floor and the underside of his chin hit the rim of the glass. He cried, and Mary immediately picked him up and held him. He kept crying, and Mary shifted him from one hip to the other. That was when she noticed that she was covered with blood. She wasn't aware that Mark was cut under the chin. The cut was a bad looking; she could see fat and meat under the skin and it was very dark, but the bleeding slowed after a while. Mary and I were not trained in any kind of medicine, but we both knew a little first aid, so we bandaged the wound up and loaded him in the car for the drive to the Two Harbors hospital emergency room.

They took us in, looked at the cut and said it needed stitches. They wrapped Mark in a sheet to immobilize his arms as they laid him on the examining table. They suggested that we leave the room while they stitched him up. Mark screamed in sheer terror, afraid of the hospital staff in white coats and that we were leaving him. We left the room listening to his cries and felt terrible. I felt so bad, it was like we were abandoning him and he was screaming for us not to leave him. It took ten stitches to sew him up, and they told us that he would be sore for a few days and should watch for infection. We took him home, did as the staff requested, and he healed up nicely but still has the scar on his chin today.

For years, whenever we would go to where people wore white clothes, such as a waiters in restaurants or the butcher at the meat counter in a grocery store, Mark would break out crying, remembering the time when he was stitched up. He associated their white coats with the pain and terror of the hospital emergency room.

MARY, LOUIE, AND LONDON SPRING
Summer 1968

ON THE ROAD UP THE BEAVER RIVER and toward the west, way past the Silver Bay Airport, is a place called London Spring. At the spring, the water flowed out of a pipe stuck in a hillside. County Highway 3 went right past it, and the story was told that in the old days, when this was the only road up along Lake Superior, the stage coaches and early automobiles used to stop here to rest and water their horses and refresh themselves. The water was cold and delicious, and the spring never stopped running. Mary and I used to travel to the London Spring as we picked agates along the gravel road. We also got water from there to make our home brew beer and wine. It was excellent for that purpose and made some pretty good booze. It wasn't too bad drinking the water straight out of the pipe either. Louie said he would like to see this place as it sounded very interesting.

We all piled into the car and headed out to the spring. When we got there, we hadn't passed another car coming or going. I just parked a little off to the side of the road as we all got out to see the spring. After we looked around the place awhile and all had a drink, we started to get into the car to leave. Louie had gotten his shoes muddy and was cleaning them off, standing on the driver's side with the back door wide open. I heard a loud noise like a truck coming down the road. When I looked up, sure enough a very large logging truck was bearing down on our car, with Louie standing in the middle of the road hanging on to the door, cleaning his shoes. I hollered for him to get in the car, but he didn't seem to hear me. I yelled again for him to get in and close the door. At the very last second, he jumped in just as the truck rumbled by. We were surprised, the trucker was surprised, and Louie got out of the way just in time.

First-Class BM Leon Woodard on the left and SN Mike Roberts in their dress whites waiting for an inspection party to arrive at Split Rock, summer 1967. (Photo Mary Roberts)

CHAPTER SIX

PEOPLE AND ANIMALS
OF SPLIT ROCK

NEW YEAR'S EVE
1967

THE TOWN SILVER BAY WAS a few miles north of Split Rock. It was the closest town with a grocery store and all of the services a family could want or need. Reserve Mining Company was located on the shore of the lake, and the company's taconite pelletizing plant was located on either side of Highway 61 at Silver Bay. They mined the taconite ore at the Peter Mitchell mine in Babbitt about sixty-five miles inland and shipped it to Silver Bay for further processing. Before I enlisted in the Coast Guard in 1966, I lived in Ely. I worked at the Babbitt mine before going into the service, and when I got out of the service, I was going back to my job at the mine.

A couple of high school friends, Jim Porthan and Richard "Buckshot" Grahek worked as plant protection at Reserve Mining in Silver Bay. On occasion when going to Silver Bay, I would stop and visit them at the plant entrance main gate guard shack and shoot the breeze, if they were on duty. I was also friends with the guys who owned and ran Zups grocery store in the shopping center. We had hung around and played sports together while in high school at Ely. Bernard was a 1959 classmate, and Ed was a couple of years older than we were. The Zupancich family owned a string of grocery stores all over the Arrowhead of northeastern Minnesota. Each store provide employment for as many of the family members who wanted to work there and many others from the communities of Silver Bay, Ely, Tower, Babbitt, and Hoyt Lakes/Aurora. The Zupanciches were a great bunch of people who always gave back to the town and community. Bernard and I and his cousins Bill and Pat all hung around in high school, played sports, partied, chased girls, hunted, fished and trapped together during our youth. Sandy Elfing, Bernie's wife, was a couple of years younger than we were, from Ely too and a lot of fun.

When Bernie and Sandy found out that we were stationed at Split Rock, they invited us over to their house on New Years Eve 1967. We thought it was a house party at the Zups, which was right up our alley because we were broke as usual. We did have enough gas to make it to Silver Bay and back home again with a little to spare. We got all spruced up and were looking forward to seeing their house and having a night of fun and frolic. We arrived on time and were they greeted warmly, but we wondered where the other people were. We had a few drinks and snacks, talked about old times and wondered, and still no other people arrived. They then asked us if we were ready to go uptown to party. Whoa! We thought this was a house party where they would supply the food and drinks. No way could we afford to go to a bar.

I had a couple of dollars on me, and that was it. We hadn't expected to go up town. Had we known, we probably would have turned down the invitation. Well, it was too late now to come off looking like a cheap skate and a piker, so up town we went. We stopped at the municipal liquor store and bar where the party was going on and sat at a table where Bernie ordered the first round. I saw that it cost about what I had in my pocket. I bought the next round, and Mary, who was not much of a drinker, could see the situation we were in, didn't have one. I was just able to cover the round. Bernie ordered and paid for the next round, as we laughed and told stories about each other. When it came to my turn to order the next round, I leaned over and whispered in his ear, asking if I could borrow $5.00. He very discretely took a $5.00 bill and passed it under the table to me. I took it and ordered the next round. About that time it was midnight. We hugged, kissed, and danced the New Year in, and then it was time to go home. Bernie saved me from the public embarrassment of not having any money, and it was never brought up in any of our further associations.

It took me about three months to come up with enough money to repay him, and we never went out again while stationed at Split Rock. When you have money, you assume that everyone else does too, but when you have no money, you also assume that everyone else has a lot more that you do, and that's usually true unless you hang out with paupers or servicemen with families.

Bernie, Ed, and I played hockey on the city teams of Silver Bay and Two Harbors and had many good times together and are still friends to this day.

LENS NIGHT OUT
SPRING OR SUMMER OF 1967

SPLIT ROCK WAS AN ISOLATED, out-in-the-boonies light station a long way from the headquarters in Duluth. We didn't have many visits from our military superiors. Group Duluth from time to time would call a meeting at the Duluth Coast Guard station for all of the officers in charge from the outlying duty stations such as Split Rock, Two Harbors, Grand Marais, Bayfield, Superior Entry, Devils Island, and the rest. On the appointed day and pre-arranged time in the designated place, all the men would meet to cover the chosen subject of the day. Safety, operations, and personnel matters were usually discussed at length. The officers in charge were mostly chiefs, first- and second-class petty officers who chose the Coast Guard as their life's work. A special bond of camaraderie existed between the older members. They were used to being together with their shipmates, as most of the career petty officers had spent a considerable amount of time on ships at sea. Being on small stations with few personnel was not the duty they looked forward to. They considered the small duty stations as being part of the on-going career path, but many of them preferred to be on larger stations with more people around. Such was the case with Len Woodard, so when he got together with his peers, they usual ended up celebrating the occasion by going out on the town and having a few drinks.

In the summer of 1967 on a bright sunny day, it was my turn to shut off the light in the morning. As I left my house and walked out through the gate out front, I saw the Coast Guard Jeep parked a little crooked in front of the Woodard's house. The door passenger's side door was hanging open, and on the ground from the Jeep to the house were groceries scattered all over the side walk and yard. I went up to the light tower and shut off the light and closed out yesterday's log entry and started the daily log for the new day. After checking to see that everything was ship shape, I went back down and out the office door and walked back toward my house.

The Woodard's yard was still untouched, with groceries everywhere, so I got some empty paper bags from on my back porch and bagged up the wayward groceries and left them on the cement walk by their house. I went about doing my daily chores. We had many things to do around the lighthouse such as cut grass, sweep the walks, paint and clean but there was no specific time frame in which to do them. When the grass was long, cut it, when the walk needed attention, sweep it, when the lighthouse windows were dirty, clean them. The officer in charge usually assigned the weekly tasks but most of the time we'd just do what needed attention. We were responsible for own quarters, garages, and lawns, but we would both do the common areas of work either together or separately. It was kind of how I would imagine a farm would work—do what needs to be done when it needs doing.

After a day or so, Woodard came out of his house to go to work around the place, and I asked him what had happened on the trip to headquarters. He said things went pretty good at the meeting. After it broke up, he went shopping at the Duluth Air Force Base Commissary, and then he got together with a bunch of guys and went out for a few drinks. Len and Dick Salison, the officer in charge of Two Harbors Light Station, rode to the meeting together and partied their way back up the North Shore.

After a night of tall tales of the old days washed down with more booze than they cared to admit, Len dropped off Salison at home, and then headed for Split Rock. When he got home, he was a bit unsteady, and the grocery bags ripped open, as some of the frozen food had thawed and got the bags wet, spilling the groceries all over the ground between the Jeep and his porch. Dress whites were the uniform of the day, so as he was picking up meat, he got blood all over his snow-white jumper and thought he got cut during the party and was bleeding to death. We had a good laugh over that.

I don't recall how much food he said got spoiled as it sat in the hot Jeep while he partied, but Len was in the dog house for quite a few days. His wife, Doris, looked down on such behavior. It sets a bad example for the kids, and she didn't want them influenced by a drunken sailor's antics even if it was their dad. Len was a neat guy and was ever so sorry for that escapade to town. He was usually such a straight arrow. I don't believe he ever did that again while he and I were stationed at Split Rock.

MARY WINS AT BINGO & FODOR GENEROSITY
JULY 1967

MARY AND DORIS WENT TO TWO HARBORS to play bingo at one of the local clubs downtown. The bingo games were held on just about any night of the week, so if they wanted to try their luck, they could find a place to play. The girls didn't get out very much, so they were really excited to go. Doris never said say how much money she had to spend, but Mary had one dollar to play as many games as she could. She was usually quite lucky at bingo, and that night, her luck held out. She won $30.00. One would have thought she'd won the lottery, she was so happy. With a baby on the way, it meant a lot of baby clothes, and maybe a new maternity top, too.

A few days after Mary won at bingo, we got a big box from Mary and Louie and family in Detroit. Upon opening it, we discovered brand new baby clothes, cloth

Doris Woodard and her mother, Anna Moses, standing outside on the lawn at Split Rock. (Photo Doris Woodard. Used with permission)

diapers, sleepers, blankets, baby toys, and just about anything a baby would need. We just couldn't believe our good fortune. It was Christmas in the middle of summer, how thoughtful of Mary's parents. A couple of days later, we got another big box. In it was a brand new baby buggy, courtesy of our baby's maternal grandparents. When you don't have very much, you can be happy, but with all of the new baby things, we were ecstatic and felt very rich. Mary and Louie didn't have very much themselves, but were very generous and helped us in our time of need.

FROSTY THE DOG
SPRING 1967

DORIS WOODARD'S DOG WAS A WHITE POODLE name Frosty. It was a kind of a jumpy lap dog like most small poodles. Frosty was part of their family and was treated like it a human. They gave it special treats and talked to it like it was a baby. She was Doris's dog but the kids were attached to it too, as they'd had it for a long time. Somehow, the dog got in to some poison set out by the neighbors to keep down the mice and died. The Woodard family was devastated. Now, what do you do with the family pet that has just expired? You give it all the respect it had while it was living by holding a funeral

Frosty, the Woodard's family dog. (Photo Doris Woodard. Used with permission)

and burying it. It would bring closure to a pet's life and give them a sense of dignity in its passing especially to the kids.

On the northeast side of the third garage—the garage that burned down—we dug a grave and laid the deceased creature to rest and erected a homemade cross over its resting place. Len said a few comforting words in Frosty's eulogy and with some tears, the kids accepted the dog's departure. Doris had a little more of a problem with its passing.

PLAYING CARDS WITH LEN & DORIS
WINTER 1967

THE WOODARDS WERE VERY NICE PEOPLE from New Bern, North Carolina. Len was a career Coastguardsman with the rank of first-class boatswain mate and took the officer in charge job at Split Rock because he wanted it. Doris was very pleasant and loved her family, her dog, and her Buick Rivera. She wasn't real thrilled about being stationed at Spilt Rock as she was a social person who thought they were out in the middle of nowhere, and she was right, they were. They had two darling little girls, Cheryl and Terry. Cheryl started school in Silver Bay, and Terry was left behind as she was a year younger. Both the kids were well mannered, and we babysat them from time to time.

Len and Doris invited Mary and me over to play cards on Saturday nights. They were good players and fun to be around. Len was a deliberate thinker, and Doris was a hurry-up kind of player. They would banter back and forth during the game, and if Doris played something other than what was in her partner's best interest, Len would say, "Doris Jean," which would get her to talking fast and calling him, "Leon T. Woodard." We had some great card games and had a lot of fun too.

Len made chief, and the billet at Split Rock called for a first class so they were transferred to Bayfield for a while and then went to Port Huron, Michigan, where Len served on a mobile boarding team. We stopped to see them once in Port Huron and again looked them up in New Bern, North Carolina, when we were on our way to Disney world in Florida in 1976. Nice people those Woodards.

CHERYL WOODARD TAKING THE BUS TO SCHOOL
WINTER 1967

CHERYL WOODARD WAS IN KINDERGARTEN when we were stationed at Split Rock. The bus would come down Highway 61 from Silver Bay to pick her up. Doris would

Cheryl Woodard getting on the school bus to go to elementary school in Silver Bay. (Photo Doris Woodard. Used with permission)

drive her out to the main road where they would wait in the car for the bus to show up. At the end of the day, she would drive out to the road to pick Cheryl up again and bring her back home. Cheryl attended elementary school in Silver Bay and was quite happy to be going to school. Younger sister Terry, on the other hand, missed her sister and playmate and wanted to go to school too, but she was too young. She never got a chance to go to school in Silver Bay with her sister as the family was transferred to Bayfield, Wisconsin, before she became of age.

THE NUNS WALK INTO OUR HOUSE
SUMMER 1967

MARY AND I WERE SITTING ON THE front porch swing we'd gotten from Goodwill in Duluth. The front porch overlooked the lake. As we talked rocked back and forth, enjoying the intermittent sun, talking about our future and the upcoming birth of our first child, we heard some noise inside our house. It sounded like people talking. I got up from the swing and went inside to investigate. What I discovered was probably the last thing I'd expect to invade my house. I mean I was prepared to turn off a radio we'd left on or find Cheryl and Terry visiting us. Nope. I found five or six Catholic nuns in full black-and-white habits walking around in our home. I asked them what they were doing. They smiled and replied that they were taking the tour.

Tour? I couldn't believe people would think they could just walk into someone's house and look around. When I told them that this was our private home and wasn't open to the public, they were very apologetic and sorry for trespassing. Mary came in and said it was okay, that it was just a mistake. We asked them to leave. As they were leaving, they inquired about Lake Superior agates and had we ever found any around

Our Split Rock quarters as taken from the entrance to the lighthouse grounds. (Photo Doris Woodard. Used with permission)

Split Rock. I told them that we picked, polished and made jewelry agates from local stones, but the best place to find them was on the beaches. They were excited and asked if they could see some of the rocks we had. Being rock hounds and proud of what we found, took out boxes of our tumbled and polished agates. They so appreciated seeing our collection, they thanked us profusely. We gave them a few agates to take with them. That really excited them. You'd have thought we gave them gold and silver, they were so happy. All told, they spent about an hour with us. I hope they liked their "tour."

LOTS OF TOURISTS COMING AND GOING
SUMMER 1967

MANY TOURISTS VISITED THE LIGHTHOUSE during the summer season. As Mary and I were sitting at our kitchen table having lunch on Memorial Day 1967, we decide to count the people who walked to the lighthouse for one hour. We counted just the people coming in, not going back out. During that lunch hour, we counted nearly 2,000 people. It was like they'd gotten off of a bus, there were so many. They just kept coming. As the visitors came to the lighthouse, if I was out in the yard either working or just hanging out, they would stop by and want to talk. Some wanted a tour of the lighthouse, but we didn't give tours.

One morning as I shut off the light, some tourists begged for a tour of the tower so I said, "Okay, it's was early and I have lots of time today. Let's go. "

We went up, and they looked around. After a while they were satisfied and ready to go down the stairs to the office and exit from the tower. We came down, and they thanked me as they were leaving through the office doors. Well, other visitors saw these folks leaving, and they asked for *their* tour. They were American citizen and taxpayers, and I'd given those other people a tour, so weren't they entitled to a tour also? I was young and dumb so I said, "Okay, let's go. "

When these next people were done with their tour, don't you know, there were more people who wanted to see the inside of the lighthouse tower. Soon I was leading tours up and down the tower all morning long. I could hardly take a break to go to the bathroom. At lunch time, I stopped giving tours to go and eat lunch and didn't go outside for quite a while. Any time after that trapped tour experience, when anyone wanted a tour, I would tell them we just didn't do that any more. I felt kind of bad about not helping them enjoy the lighthouse to the fullest, but giving tours really wasn't in my job description, and I had many things to do. If I gave tours, I wouldn't have time to do anything else.

On occasion, at the end of the day or the end of the season, if I had time, I would give a tour if someone specifically asked me. Fewer people were around than at the height of the season. I could put myself in their shoes, and I know if I were them I'd like to see how a lighthouse operated.

VISITORS TO SPLIT ROCK

W HEN THE SNOW FLEW AT SPLIT ROCK, visitations were few. Most of the people who stopped in to see the lighthouse were usually on vacation. There aren't too many vacations taken in the winter up north. Minnesotans tend to go south where it's warm. We kept the roads and walkways clear of ice and snow, but it was just so we could get around the place. However, when it started to warm up around April and we turned the light back on for the season, it seemed to draw the visitors like moths to a flame. It was mainly on weekends that they showed up to see the lighthouse, but as it got closer to Memorial Day, the trickle of visitors became a torrent. At times, there were so many cars arriving that the parking lot out in front of the gift shop was full. They then parked along the blacktop road coming in. Our residence on the property was like living in a fish bowl. However, everyone usually seemed to be in a pretty good mood depending on the weather, and the summers passed rather quickly.

PEOPLE LOCKING THEMSELVES OUT OF THEIR CARS . . . ALL THE TIME

MORE THAN ONCE PEOPLE WOULD KNOCK on our door and ask to use our bathroom or request if we could help them get into their cars. If it was to use the bath room, that was an easy one. We pointed them to the gift shop where there were facilities just for visitors. It was off to the left of their building and very busy for most of the summer. We supplied the gift shop with water, and it seemed like our pump was running all of the time, especially on weekends and holidays.

If the request was to help them get into their cars because they had locked their keys inside, that was a different story. I wasn't very good at breaking into cars when first asked but I got better as time went on. I had been asked so many times to help that I had my car break-in burglar tools hanging on the wall in my garage. A straightened out coat hanger with a hook or loop on the end seemed to work most of the time. By pushing the hooked or looped end down through the gasket around the window and hook it around the door locking knob and pull it up was the most common method of entry. Sometime I'd hook the door handle and pull it up. That seemed to work well on a variety of cars. If the keys were left in the ignition and I couldn't hook the locking knob or pull up on the handle, it was almost impossible to get it open without a Slim Jim, a tool that police and burgerlers use to break into cars. I didn't have one of those. A few times when it was impossible to open the door and the cops or the locksmith couldn't or wouldn't come to help, the owners would opt to break a window to gain entry. I wouldn't break anyone's window. I'd tell them how, and they would break it. It was a hard learned and expensive lesson in forgetfulness.

TALKING TO THE LIGHTHOUSE KEEPER'S DAUGHTER
SUMMER 1968

DURING THE SUMMERS, THOUSANDS OF PEOPLE visited the lighthouse as it was so accessible from the highway. Highway 61 was the principal road along Lake Superior. People came from all over the United States and the world to see the scenery of the north shore. Whenever we were outside doing routine summer maintenance, visitors wanted to stop and talk about the lighthouse. Being the social guy that I am, I also enjoyed talking to them as well. They would ask all the usual lighthouse questions, and I'd give all the usual lighthouse answers, then I'd ask a few questions of my own, so it was give and take.

One beautiful summer day, I was tending the flower garden below the entrance sign, when a lady in her late sixties or early seventies stopped to chat on her way in to see the lighthouse. She said that her dad had been a lighthouse keeper at Split Rock many years ago when she was a little girl. Split Rock had once been her home. We talked as I continued to work on the flowers. As I had caught up on my weeding, she said she was going up to see if the lighthouse had changed over the years. I walked with her toward the lighthouse. We talked on the way, and when we rounded the corner and the lighthouse came into view, she almost shouted, "You painted the bottom white." I said that it had been white the whole time I had been stationed there. She said that it used to be black. The part of the lighthouse she was talking about was the bottom of the office part of the lighthouse. She mentioned that she was from Michigan's Upper Peninsula and they were just passing through on a site seeing trip to Port Arthur and Fort William at Thunder Bay. I now wish I had gotten her name and what town she was from but with so many daily visitors, it didn't seem important at that time.

THE INSPECTOR AND POCO THE DOG
MID-SUMMER 1968

DURING MY TENURE AT SPLIT ROCK LIGHTHOUSE, we didn't have too much direction or interference from the Group Duluth Headquarters or, for that matter, the Ninth Coast Guard District Office out of Cleveland, Ohio. We rarely ever saw any one at Split Rock who was connected to the Coast Guard except on special occasions, such as light station inspections. The Split Rock officer in charge usually attended meetings at group Duluth headquarters on Park Point to get the lowdown on what the newest regulations and instructions were.

I was not the officer in charge at any time during my stay at Split Rock but was the assistant who, as the station seaman, followed orders. During Second-Class Boatswains Mate Bruce Robb's time at Split Rock, an admiral from the Cleveland Headquarters of the Ninth District came for an inspection. Robb informed me that an inspection was going to take place, and we had to get the station spruced up and looking extra special. So we painted and polished, groomed, trimmed and cut everything that needed it in advance of the admiral's arrival. On the day of the inspection, Robb and I were in our dress whites and proud of the way the light station looked, and we were ready to show it off.

The admiral arrived at the designated time, and we met him and his party with salutes and hand shakes all around. He inquired as to our satisfaction with our job at Split Rock and the Coast Guard in general. He was an elderly gentleman—like most admirals—and at the top of his career. He probably wanted to get out of the hubbub of the headquarters and do a little fishing and sightseeing. He couldn't have picked a better way to relax than to go on an inspection tour of remote Coast Guard installations up on the north shore of Lake Superior, "God's County" as some called it.

Robb and I walked the admiral and his company around the grounds and up through the lighthouse. As the inspection team was winding down their tour and heading for the entrance, the old man said he would like to inspect the living quarters of the station personnel. We hadn't expected that he was interested in seeing our quarters. Mary had our house spic and span, in top notch shape as always as she was an excellent housekeeper. She had put in a little extra effort, just in case they might want to do a walk through. Robb's wife, Kathy, worked in Duluth so their house, never had a chance to get messy, but they had a small black poodle name Poco.

As the admiral and everyone in the inspection party, myself included, walked through Robb's house, the admiral remarked at the great condition of the place, even

SN Mike Roberts (left) and Second-Class BM Bruce Robb, waiting for the inspectors to arrive at Split Rock in the summer of 1968. (Photo Kathy Robb. Used with permission)

if was built many years ago. Going from room to room and observing the general up-keep of the home, the admiral stopped to look out the window. On the floor, below the window, Poco had left a big pile of dog crap. Robb, in his haste to make a good impression, never thought to check his house for any thing amiss. After all, Poco was part of the family, and they treated him like a baby. The admiral after looking out the window and slowly turning away to go to the next room said, "Oh, I see you have a dog" and without further ado or missing a beat, continued on his inspection tour. The admiral had to be the coolest old guy in the Coast Guard. I'll bet he told that dog crap experience story for many years right into his retirement. When the inspection was completed, the admiral and inspection party a distant memory, we had a good laugh at the unexpected antics of Poco, the dog.

HOME BREW PARTY
Fall 1968

BRUCE ROBB, THE OFFICER IN CHARGE, and his wife, Kathy, didn't much like the iso-lation of the Split Rock Lighthouse as Kathy worked in Duluth and Bruce was a city guy from a suburb near Chicago. They were young and liked to be where the action was, and there wasn't much going on at Split Rock as it was pretty laid back. On the other hand, Jim and Carol Schubert were from the farming country near Mineral Point, Wisconsin, and liked being out in the boonies. Prior to coming to Minnesota's north shore in Two Harbors, they were stationed in Alaska. Robb and Schubert both being officer's in charge of light stations and about the same rank, thought they might "mu-tual" to a duty station more to their liking.

Mutualing was when personnel of the same rank and rate would change duty stations without getting a set of orders from headquarters. They just got permission from the commanding officer. The commander of Group Duluth, Lieutenant George Bannon, usually didn't care who filled the billet just as long as they were close to the same rank and rate. Rank was the level of your responsibility such as E-3, E-4, E-5, and so forth. Rate was what your specialty was in the service such as yoeman, boatswain, and engineman. When the personnel changed duty stations on a mutual, it was at no cost to the Coast Guard. The people mutualling picked up all of the costs of the transfer themselves including travel and moving expenses. They just exchanged duty stations.

Schuberts came up to Split Rock to see if it would be a compatible place for them to transfer to and see if they would like Mary and me for neighbors and as a coworker.

When they showed up, it was unannounced. We had no idea they were coming for a visit. Jim and I walked around the station, and I showed him what he was getting into. He liked what he saw. In the meantime, Carol and Mary visited in the house. Mary was pregnant with our second child, Eric, and Carol was pregnant with their soon to be born, Mike. Our Mark was just a little guy about fourteen months old, so the girls had plenty to talk about. Home, kids, husbands, and duty stations were just some of the topics of the day.

When Jim and I came back into the house, Mary asked the Schuberts to stay for supper. She was about to make supper before the Schuberts arrived but only had about half a pound of hamburger. As luck would have it, chili was on the menu, and Mary being the resourceful cook she that she is, added more beans and broth to make it stretch into a supper for four.

In the meantime, Bruce and Kathy Robb came home, so we invited them over too. Mary added more beans and broth and stretched the meal for two into a dinner for six. She whipped up some biscuits and took care of Mark at the same time. When the supper was served, we had chili, salad, biscuits, and a freshly baked cake. It was delicious and there was plenty for everyone. After eating, I asked if they would like to try some home-brewed beer. The brew that I had been aging for the last month in the storage room under the basement steps was just about reaching the time for consumption. I had made about ten gallons, and it was neatly stacked on the shelves aging in the dark.

When I opened the door to the storage room and turned on the light, the amber liquid in clear glass pop bottles looked just like it was Miller High Life except for the screw on caps dipped in wax. I brought up three bottles, one for each family and explained that this was my first attempt at making home brew. Everyone laughed and said it looked great and hoped it tasted half as good as it looked.

Inside, on the bottom of the bottle, was thin coating of yeast which Jim called "mother," and he explained that it was a residue from the yeast but not to worry as it didn't affect the taste unless you emptied the bottle clear down to the bottom. The guys filled their glasses and tasted the beer. "It tastes great" was the general verdict. I was happy that my first attempt was successful, that I had someone to share it with, and it was lot cheaper than the store-bought stuff.

We drank the first round but Mary and Carol didn't have any as they were pregnant. The guys asked, "Do you have any more?"Being a proud brewer, I said, "Sure," and went down to my private stash and got three more bottles. When I brought the second round up, it looked as good as or possibly better than the first,. We proceeded to polish this next batch off which led to another trip to the basement to get some more. We talked about duty stations, boot camp, the Vietnam War, search-and-rescue missions and lighthouses. I brought out my guitar, and we sang, laughed, told stories and jokes and drank more beer. By the time the night was over, we had downed about three or four gallons, didn't really care if we drank the "mother" in the bottom of the bottles or not, sang all the songs we knew, told endless jokes and sea stories and ate up just about everything we had in the house that wasn't frozen.

It was a great spur-of-the-moment, one-to-remember party, and all of us guys got roaring drunk. When it was time to go home, well after midnight, Kathy helped Bruce walk to their house next door, and he laid low for a couple of days. I don't remember going to bed that night, and I had the damndest hangover, which lasted two days before I felt right again. Carol drove Jim home to a house full of smoke.

As it turned out, when they had come to Split Rock that afternoon, it was going to be just for an hour or so, just a quick meet and greet. Carol left some soup on the stove cooking slow on low heat at the Two Harbors Light Station and forgot all about it. When they got home, the soup had completely cooked away and burned the contents of the pot into a grimy smoke that covered the whole inside of their home. They decided that a move to Split Rock would be a good one, so they mutualed with the Robbs. But before they left the Two Harbors Light Station, they had to repaint the whole inside of their house due to the smoke from the burned up soup. Whenever we get together, we still laugh about the home brew beer party and their first Split Rock Lighthouse visit.

BRUCE ROBB, FURNITURE MAKER
Winter 1967-1968

DURING THE FALL OF 1968 WHEN BRUCE ROBB was stationed at Split Rock, he bought a Craftsman ten-inch radial arm saw with all of the attachments and set it up in his basement. It was a marvelous machine that could cut just about any angle desired. He got very proficient using it and made a round-top cedar chest for one of his close relatives. It not only had a round top but was tapered at both ends. It looked like a pirate's chest with copper hinges and fancy hardware. It was quite a feat for a novice woodworker. I don't recall if he made it from a pattern or just did it as a spur-of-the-moment project, but it turned out beautifully. He also made a set of bookshelves out a four-by-eight sheet of finished plywood with that same saw. It looked professionally built upon completion. Bruce always had a special project going in his basement over the winter of 1967-1968.

A Moose in Two Harbors

As Highway 61 heads out of town up the shore, just past County Highway 2 and on the left behind the Holiday store is a building that, in the late 1960s, was a service club. I don't recall which one. As Mary and I were driving back to Split Rock, we passed the club and we couldn't believe our eyes. In the strip of lawn between the club and the highway was a great big moose. We remarked to one another that it sure looked like a real moose, figuring it must be a statue someone had put on the lawn for a joke. They'd made it particularly lifelike. A curious people by nature, we had to turn around and go back to check it out again. That's when it moved. Sure enough, it was a real live moose standing on the lawn right in Two Harbors. It seemed that a wild moose had wandered out of the woods and happened to be standing on the lawn right in the middle of town just as we went by. It hung around for a while and then meandered on its way. While having moose show up on the North Shore wasn't rare exactly, having one wander right into town really wasn't the norm. Sometimes strange things happened in the darnedest places at the most unexpected times

Hibernating Flies
Winter 1967

In the winter after the shipping season was done for the year and the light was shut off until spring, we didn't go up into the light tower very often as there was nothing there that needed our attention in the off season. There was no heat in the tower, so when it got cold outside, it was also just as cold inside. In midwinter, when it was well below zero, I climbed up the circular stairs to the top of the light tower just to check things out.

As I went up, on the left of the stairs was a window that was just about head high. I usually looked at the thickness of the tower wall and the condition of the paint in the window well. In the upper right hand corner of this window was a tight knot of black house flies. The clump was about the one-fourth the size of a clenched fist. They were all tightly entwined together. I had to look closely at the black ball to figure out what it was. I had never seen anything like that before. They were hibernating and frozen stiff. I had no idea where they came from. I had never noticed any flies around when it was warm out. I also wondered why they picked that particular window as there were many others to choose from. I went on my inspection of the upper lighthouse and on my way back down, I scooped them up and threw them out in to the freezing cold weather. I didn't want a bunch of flies coming to life when summer came back to the lighthouse.

Chapter Seven

The Buildings and Machines of Split Rock

The Machinery of the Lighthouse

GOING UP THE STEPS OF THE FACE of the rock toward the lighthouse tower, turning right and going up a few more steps will bring one to the lighthouse office. Going through the office door, the Kohler light plant is on the right and was set up to start automatically when the electricity from the power company was lost. The engine was painted gray, and on the top of the radiator the name KOHLER was cast into the housing. We would run it from time to time to make sure that, when it was needed, it would start every time. On occasions, when the power did go off, it performed flawlessly each and every time.

Against the west wall under the windows was the steel office desk with a rolling swivel chair centered in the space between the generator and the south wall. On the desk was the station log in which all the happening of the day were recorded. Some of the things we wrote about were the weather conditions at the time of writing, any thing that had happened in the day out of the ordinary, the transfer of station personnel and the turning on and off of the light on a daily basis. The time to turn the light on and off changed every day as the season lengthened and shortened. There was a chart on the south wall of the office that gave the exact time of the Duluth sunrise

97

and sunset on any given day of the year. We used that information to turn the light on and off. Turning the light on was of paramount importance and the reason for the lighthouse's existence. We always made sure it was always turned on one half hour before sun set. The only vessels that used the light any more were small boats, as the larger ships had radio beacons for navigation. The Coast Guard kept the station open just for public relations or so the story goes. However, the small boats still might need the light to find their way to safety.

The shipping season generally started around the middle to the end of March or the beginning of April. This event was always well publicized by the media, and it changed with the weather and ice conditions, but it was also driven by the steel industry and shipping companies. The Coast Guard Cutter *Mackinaw* was usually sent across the lake from Sault Saint Marie to open a channel to get the season underway. The media would always cover this event of the changing seasons. The top brass from Coast Guard Group Duluth would notify us in advance so we could get the light ready for action. We then followed, with dedication, the main task of a lighthouse keeper, making sure that light shined all night, every night, and was on time for the next eight or nine months until the shipping season ended. We generally secured the light for the season around Christmas or just before, again depending on the weather conditions. If the lake froze up early, then the light was shut off to reflect that early freeze up. I can't imagine what the old sailors who were "Iron men in wooden ships" did to stay warm on those, late-season crossings.

We logged the daily weather at the time of writing the log. It was the observation of the man on duty with an estimation of wind speed and direction and the general weather conditions as to sunny, raining, snowing, and that sort of thing. Reading the log, I could see when keepers came and went, as well as odd happenings. Turning off the light in the morning, however, was not considered an act of importance, after all, we kept everyone away from danger and safe all night with our beacon. That was our real job.

There were only two of us regular coastguardsmen on station as permanent staff, and we rotated the duty. It was the man on duty's responsibility to turn the light on and off. If it didn't get shut off within a half an hour after sunrise, what was the harm? Just the electricity it took to revolve the light and the juice to keep it lit. There were times when we would shut the light off at 8:00 A.M., when we would go to work. When the sun was down, the lighthouse structure was the visible means of lake vessels' location as it could be seen from a great distance. But really, other than maintainance of the light and tower, there wasn't very much going on at the lighthouse on any given day.

During the day, the sunlight coming through the windows gave the lighthouse a very open and spacious feeling. The inside walls were ceramic tile that was easy to wipe down and keep clean but reflected sound, producing a kind of an echo throughout the tower. At night, if I had to go up to the lighthouse for any reason, it was a little on the spooky side. The light would revolve in a clockwise direction three times a minute, and there was a very distinct clicking noise from time to time during the revolutions. That clicking noise would sound throughout the whole lighthouse . With the echo effect, it kind of gave me the willies. I did not see any ghosts or hear any of my predecessors speak of any such occurrences but the lighthouse at night was an eerie place of shadows, sounds, and my own apprehension. Very rarely did I have to go up to the lighthouse at night alone, and that was okay by me. It wasn't that I was scared of the place, but just a bit apprehensive of what a person might see or think they saw. Quite frankly, I think we're all a little more impressionable at night.

Walking down the passageway from the office to the light tower was just a few paces, and there was nothing of note in this hallway—it was just a hall way. At the end of the hallway, it opened up into the base of the tower. The steel, circular, gray stairway with its handrail wound up the side of the tower. From the top of the lighthouse down to the floor of the ground floor, in the dead center of the room, was a steel tube that was also painted gray and housed the weight that actually turned the light before it was powered by electricity. The weights were suspended on a cable and were pulled down by gravity. This force caused the light to revolve, kind of like the mechanism of a grandfather clock.

The circular steel stairs were mounted on the inside of the outer walls of the tower starting in the southeast and winding up to the lantern deck. After climbing the stairs to the lantern deck, a door leads to the machinery of the lighthouse. The winch to raise the weights that caused the light to revolve was on the right side of the walkway.

It was encased in a wood-and-glass enclosure with a hole in the side to insert the hand crank to wind up the winch. Inside the case was the governor with its set of brass balls that set the speed of the descending weights. That speed was set to produce three revolutions per minute which cause it to be a ten-second light. Each time the lens revolved 360 degrees, it would flash twice, once from one side of the clam-shaped lens and once from the other.

On the lantern deck rested the base of the reservoir that held the mercury on which the actual base of the light floated effortlessly. The winch was no longer in use during my time of service, having been replaced by an electric motor rotating the light. The steps from the lantern deck went up to the next level which was the actual light lens with the windows overlooking the lake.

The curved glass panels of the windows were placed to face the lake and the light shone at about 200-plus degrees. The steel panels on the back side of the light tower stopped the light from shining into the quarters and the surrounding woods around the houses.

There was a man door on the northwest side that opened out on to the catwalk. It seemed that every time I opened the door to go outside at the top of the lighthouse, the wind was always blowing. The only task that needed doing on the outside catwalk was cleaning the windows, and that was done from time to time as needed. I'm happy to say that the catwalk and the roof of the light tower never needed painting while I was stationed there.

The very top of the lighthouse had a lightning rod on it. From that device ran a copper wire down the side of the stone building, and it was anchored in the bedrock. I don't ever recall a lightning storm while stationed there.

The fog signal building was empty except for the cement pads on the floor where the fog signal machinery was once located. There was an old, unused and abandoned bathroom on the left or north side of the building from the door. On the southeast end and corner of the building was an empty wooden cabinet. Woodard and I put a large yellow oil tank in the fog signal building and with some copper tubing ran it across the steps and rock to pipe it over to the lighthouse office. When Shorty would come and fill up the station's oil supply tanks, we would have him fill up the oil tank in the fog signal building, too. We had an oil burner in the office for heat in the winter and the copper tubing carrying the #1 fuel oil from the fog signal building sure beat hauling the fuel up to the lighthouse by hand.

The lighthouse was built around the turn of the twentieth century, and I was continuously impressed with the quality of the materials used in its construction. The ingenious methods used to solve the problems of building a structure on a bald rock at the top of a cliff on the edge of a huge Lake Superior were evident everywhere. Those original designers and builders were true craftsmen in every sense.

THE LIGHT AND THE LIGHT CHANGER

THE ACTUAL LIGHT FROM THE LIGHTHOUSE was about 128 feet above the water and could be seen by mariners thirty miles out. As it was a ten-second light, which meant that it flashed every ten seconds, one could time the interval between flashes. This gave the characteristic of the light, so one knew it was Split Rock. The light shined all night long from one-half hour before sunset to one-half hour after sunrise.

The part of the lighthouse facing toward the lake had a curved glass window and the back part away from the lake was black steel sheeting. As the light revolved, the lens would focus the 1,000 watt incandescent light bulb through the exact center of the bull's eye and then transfer the light to the surrounding curved prisms. The light was said to be 1,000,000 candle power which could be seen by passing ship and if conditions were right, sometimes all of the way to Wisconsin.

The incandescent light bulb for the light was very unique as it had particles of sharp crushed stones in the base where the bulb was screwed into the light holder socket.

At times, the inside of the long cylindrical light bulb would get smoked up by carbon, which would adhere to the inside wall of the glass bulb and make the light go dim. About every 100 hours, I'd climb up a ladder inside of the clam shaped lens and remove the bulb, turn it on its side as to be horizontal and slowly revolve it so the crushed stone from the bottom would clean off all the carbon build up on the sides of the bulb. After doing this cleaning, I would then reinsert the bulb into the holder, screw it back in place and it would be good for another 100 hours.

The light changer device, which held two 1,000-watt light bulbs, was located up the ladder, inside the lens. Its purpose was to automatically change a burned-out bulb with another when the time came. We always had a supply of these special bulbs on hand just in case we needed them. I don't remember the light changer ever cycling, as we kept a close eye on the bulb and its condition. If the glass of the bulb started to blister from the intense heat of the filament, we would change the bulb immediately and throw the old one away. I don't recall what they cost, but they were very expensive. The main purpose of the lighthouse was to keep the light operating, and we took our responsibility seriously.

During Woodards time at Split Rock, the Coast Guard sent a civilian contractor named Joe out with a quartz iodine light to replace the incandescent one. After he got the job done, he was going to throw the old one away. I asked him if I could have it and he said, "Okay," and gave it to me. I put it in my garage, and it stayed there until they decommissioned the light station in December of 1969. I brought the light changer device and bulbs back to Ely and stored them in my garage there for years. I had no use for it, but I just couldn't throw it away, as the gravel-filled light bulb fascinated me. When we left Ely to move to Jackson, Minnesota, in 1976, I ran across the light changer with bulbs and brought it back to Split Rock and gave it to the guy in charge. I explained who I was and how I had came by the light changer. He thanked me and said he'd store them somewhere in case they ever needed them in the future for whatever purpose. At that time there had been talk about restoring the lighthouse to its former prominence, and they might use the light changer as one of the displays or exhibits.

The Telephone System at Split Rock

When Mary and I came to Split Rock in December of 1966, there was phone in the officer in charge's quarters and one up in the lighthouse office. Whenever we needed to make a phone call for any reason, we had to use the lighthouse phone. I don't recall why, but that was just the way it was. The communication between the houses was by sound-powered phone. Anytime I wanted to call the officer in charge, I would put the phone to my ear and hold it there with my shoulder hunched up while I turned the crank on the body or cradle of the phone in a clockwise direction with the other hand. The turning motion would send a signal to the other phone and make it ring. I don't recall if there was one up in the lighthouse office, but I imagine there probably was. It was an old, odd system, but, again, that's the way it was.

After our son Mark was born, we had a regular phone installed as it was too much for Mary to have to take a new born baby up to the lighthouse office every time she wanted to make a doctor's appointment or call her family in Detroit. I also don't recall if we paid the phone bill or the Coast Guard did, but it certainly was convenient to have a phone with an outside line in our house.

When the garage burned, Jim Schubert called me on the sound-powered phone to tell me the garage was on fire and that I should call the fire department. I picked up the regular phone and called the fire department. It was in the middle of winter and the middle of the day, and the fire department was all volunteer. People had to be called at their work places, respond, get back to the station, then be deployed out to us. Even though volunteer departments still exist in many places, every fire-fighter on call now carries a cell phone so the response time is quicker. If the same fire occurred today, chances are the fire department would have been able to save the building and Jim Schubert's car. There wasn't anything that could be done to save it then.

The Quarters at Split Rock

The houses at Split Rock were brick. All three houses had been built at the same time with the same floor plans. The main floor had a kitchen, pantry, dining room, living room, telephone desk area, and front porch. Upstairs was a bathroom on the immediate left t at the top of the stairs and three bedrooms. The master bedroom was facing the lake or was on the south of the building.

The heat was hydronic hot water with cast-iron radiators in every room. The electricity was adequate with old-style push button switches to turn the light on and off. The windows were double hung and a little hard to open at times. The kitchen had a four-burner electric stove with an oven, a single-compartment cast-iron sink with a drain board on the right side, and a large modern refrigerator. The kitchen table and chairs sat under the window

Mary, Mike, and Mark on Mike's twenty-seventh birthday in our Split Rock kitchen on August 31, 1968. (Photo Mary Roberts)

on the east side of the room. We could see visitors walking by on the asphalt and saw the lighthouse tower through the kitchen window. A cabinet to the right of the kitchen sink was built to enlarge the work space of the area. There were wall-hung, white, steel cupboards over the countertop of the floor-mounted cabinets. The floors of the kitchen were covered with linoleum. The door to the basement was on the southeast side of the room.

SN Tom Grebs's living room at Split Rock Lighthouse. (Photo Doris Woodard. Used with permission)

103

Two doorways led from the kitchen to other parts of the house. One doorway was on the south wall between the stove and refrigerator, and another was on the west wall of the room, between the refrigerator and the sink. The pantry was located through the doorway on the west side of the kitchen. It was a narrow room with a small window on the north side of the house. The pantry had a flour storage bin with a bread mixing board on top. Both sides of the pantry had shelves from the floor to the ceiling where we stored can goods, dishes, cleaning supplies, brooms, and dustpan. The dining room was to the west of the pantry in the northwest corner of the house. There were heating radiators up against the north and west outside walls under the windows. In the center of the room was a dining room table with six chairs. There was a china closet hutch in the northwest corner of the dining room. The officer in charge's house was a bit fancier than the station seamen's house. As I recall, the floor was carpeted wall to wall and there was a fancy overhead light centered over the table.

Going from the dining room through a doorway to the south was the living room. The couch or davenport located there had three cushions and was made of brown leather or an imitation leather-type material. It was cold when first sat upon and then got sticky as it made a person sweat. The covering was such that it did not breathe. The chair, made of the same material, had one cushion and matched the couch. A coffee table was in front of the couch, and Mark was so proud when he could pull himself up and stand by that table. There was a corner-type table that the TV sat on and a homemade magazine rack next to the couch.

Officer in Charge Woodard's dining room at Split Rock Lighthouse. (Photo Doris Woodard. Used by permission)

Leaving the living room and going to the east was a wide hallway that had a telephone table and chair set near the doorway to the kitchen. The freezer stood in the corner close to the stairway. The stair way to the upper floor was on the east wall, the opening to the stairs was to the south. It had two landings, one, after a few steps up, had a 180-degree turn and went up to the next landing which had a ninety-degree turn, and then went to the top floor. At the top of the stairs on the left was the bathroom. It had a lavatory/sink, toilet, and a bathtub with a shower. The fixtures were white and were definitely not of the latest style. The master bedroom was straight ahead, past the bathroom, and it had two sets of windows that faced the lake. There were two radiators on the outside walls. The furniture included a dresser with a large mirror and a bed with two nightstands on either side of it. The floors throughout the second floor were hardwood.

The bedroom to the northwest had heating radiators on the outside walls and a bed with night stands but I don't recall a dresser there. In the closet on the east side of this room was a large crack on the outside wall which I monitored from time to time. It didn't seem to get any bigger but I was told to measure and record it, so I did. Nothing was done about it as I brought it to the attention of the administration so they knew it was there. The bedroom to the northeast had no furniture so we turned it into a sewing room for Mary and it eventually became the baby's room complete with a crib, small dresser and a Disney mural I painted on the south wall.

The house was warm and comfortable with plenty of windows for light and ventilation if needed. The windows throughout the house had curtains except of the kitchen and Mary sewed a set for it. Some windows had shades but I can't recall which ones. We painted the living room when we first moved in as it was an orange-tomato soup color that we just couldn't live with. The house was in excellent shape with no outstanding problems. The basement had a storage room under the steps. The hot water boiler had a side-arm domestic water heater using fuel oil. There was a work bench on the west wall. The unused cistern, which took up about an eighth of the basement space, was located in the center of the room on the north wall. The basement was a great workshop location and had plenty of room.

Something odd happened from time to time down in the basement. A deep rumbling noise would occur from underneath the floor of the house almost like a sound of the earth shifting deep down inside of the rock. It was a sound I had heard a few times while living in Detroit. A salt mine lay deep under the downriver area of Detroit. As they mined the salt, they would blast it loose late at night or early in the morning. That was the sound I heard at Split Rock.

Looking back, our living quarters were adequate, comfortable and furnished. The officer in charge, who was usually a bit older, had a household that had been established for a while and brought a lot of their stuff with them to the station. The station seaman, which was my title, had very little household furnishing to bring to Split Rock. We didn't have much time or money to accumulate much. We also knew we could be transferred at any time, and it was difficult to drag a lot of stuff with us from place to place. The government didn't pay to move lower-ranking personnel's personal belongings to the next duty station. Even though we didn't have much to bring with us to Split Rock, we were happy to be together there and the quarters were great.

THE WATER SYSTEM AT SPLIT ROCK

SPLIT ROCK LIGHTHOUSE SITS ON TOP a high rocky cliff, with the vastness of Lake Superior just beyond. So much water within view, but drinking water was difficult to obtain. Between the garage that burned down and the middle garage was a pump house. The story I heard concerning the well in the pump house was that they tried to drill though the rock many years before to find water, and but after an arduous drilling down though the rock, the water they found was brackish, so they gave up. When I was at Split Rock this well was never used.

How they solved the water problem was to drill a well at a forty-three-degree angle traveling south toward the lake to reach the water of Lake Superior. This was done many years before, but I don't know how many. The lake well casing was located in a small cellar like enclosure on the east side of the middle house. The submersible pump was inserted into the well casing and went down into the water below the lake. The line from this pump went up and into the cistern. The cisterns held rain water collected off the roof before the well was installed. The down spouts from the eaves troughs emptied into the cistern in each house.

The well pump was controlled by a micro float switch located in the cistern in the middle house. The float was attached to a long metal rod on which two movable bushings were affixed with set screws. The bushing could be moved up or down to different heights, and this controlled the on and off cycle of the submersible pump down in the well. The higher up the bushing the rod rode, the more water was pumped into the cistern. The lower the bushing, the less water got pumped.

A pipe ran through the side wall from the cistern to a centrifugal pump and pressure tank located near the cistern. The pressure tank had a pressure switch that controlled the centrifugal pump in the basement. The outlet pipe from the pressure tank ran to all of the houses and the gift shop next door. The inlet pipe from the submersible pump in the well was connected to a small injector pump. That small pump drew a liquid mixture of HTH (Chlorine) out of a twenty-gallon Red Wing crock that stood next to the injector pump. Every time the water in the cistern ran low, the bushing on the rod would drop and trip the micro-switch there by turning on the submersible pump down in the well. At the same time, when the water ran into the cistern, the injector pump would inject a small amount of liquid chlorine water into the stream of water coming up from the well. The well water and the chlorine from the HTH would be delivered to the cistern and from there to be used in the houses and gift shop.

The centrifugal pump and the eighty-gallon galvanized pressure tank sat on the floor out a few feet from the cistern entrance. The cistern entrance was about four to five feet off the floor and was a square hole about three feet by three feet. There was a painted wooden cover over the hole of the cistern. The inside of the cistern was back plastered smooth and painted with white epoxy paint or so it appeared. The water in the cistern was about four feet high at its highest level.

The water going over to the gift shop was carried in a three-quarter-inch galvanized pipe laid on the top of the ground. The pipe was installed in a joint effort between Maurice D. Francis, the gift shop owner and the Coastguardsman on duty. It was put out in the spring after the last frost and picked up again at the end of the season usually around the end of October. It stayed in place all summer. As I recall, the gift shop had a public flush toilet in a separate building to the north of the gift shop and it was used all during the tourist season.

The Coast Guard personnel had to submit a station water sample once a month. A water lab down in Duluth would send an empty bottle inside an unbreakable container by mail and the officer in charge would take the sample and send it back to the lab. During the winter of 1967, Woodard took his family back home to New Bern, North Carolina, for a leave of a month or so, and I was the only guy left on the station, making me in charge of taking the water sample and sending it off to Duluth.

In the sample bottle container was a set of implicit instructions to follow when taking the sample. One of the instructions was to heat the end of the tap or faucet to kill the bacteria that might be growing there. I thought to myself, "I wonder if they even test the water. How many bugs could possibly be living in the faucet? We drink it and don't get sick. "So I decided not to heat up the end of the faucet with the propane torch provided for that purpose, just to see what would happen. I took the sample and sent it off in the next day's mail. It didn't freeze on its way to the lab but I got an empty bottle back a short time later with instructions to be sure to sterilize the end of the tap with heat to kill the growing bacteria so they could get a good sample. Well, I'll be darned, they actually did analyze the water sample, and someone was looking out for our health and well being. I drew the water sample as instructed and sent it off to Duluth and never heard another word from the water testing lab.

CROSS CONNECTION
Early Fall 1967

ONE DAY, WHILE TAKING A SHOWER, I noticed that the water felt a little slippery, almost greasy and had an odd smell. When I told Len about it, He said, "I wonder why that would be? Let's go check it out." We went in to his basement and looked the water system over. Everything looked in order until we opened up the hatch of the cistern, and the smell hit us. It smelled like rotting garbage. We got a trouble light and looked in the cistern and saw Cheerios, small orange peelings, lettuce leaves, and other junk floating on top of our drinking water. Small bits of eggs shells and coffee grounds were below the surface. Yuck, we were drinking, bathing and cooking with sewer water. It was a wonder we all didn't get sick and die from the contamination.

Now, we had to find the cause of the problem. Len went up stairs and flushed the toilet and nothing happened, it just went down. He ran the water down the drain in the bathroom sink and tub, still nothing. Next he ran the water in the kitchen and all of that drainage water backed up and went into the cistern through the cistern overflow. The overflow pipe from the cistern was connected to the drain line from the kitchen sink and for years, no one knew it. When the drain line plugged up down near the floor, all of the kitchen sink waste water backed up and ran into the cistern through the overflow as it had no place else to go. The hidden cross connection between the fresh water supply and the waste water drain line almost spelled disaster for both families.

We shut off the shallow water pump so no water would flow to the houses. We explained to our families what had happened and what we had to do to get the water back on. The first thing we did was unclog the drain line going out to the septic tank which was located outside between the houses, cliff, and lake. When we got that horizontal drain line clear, we ran down lots of water to flush it out. We then disconnected the cistern overflow line from the kitchen sink drain line and plugged off the overflow line to the kitchen sink. We next ran the overflow line down to the floor drain and that solved those two problems.

We now had to clean out the cistern, sanitize it and make it usable again. We turned the deep well pump down in the lake well off and and turned the shallow well pump back on and pumped most of the contaminated water out of the cistern. We put a sump pump in the corner and pumped the rest of the water out of the cistern and down the floor drain. Len climbed into the cistern and began scrubbing down the walls with a Hi-Lex bleach solution, the smell was ferocious. He rinsed the walls down and washed them again until they were clean and back to the original shape. The cistern had originally been back plastered with waterproof cement which was painted with a white epoxy waterproof paint.

After the cleaning, the cistern looked pretty good and was ready to go back into service. We turned the deep well pump on and began to fill it up. After a while, the water level rose in the cistern and the automatic pump switch shut that pump off. We turned on the shallow well pump and pressurized the home water system again and everything was back to normal, we had pure drinkable running water again.

The old saying, "You never miss the water until the well runs dry," was absolutely true. We were without water only for a couple of days, but it was a colossal pain in the butt hauling it from the neighbors while we worked to fix the problem.

THE GAS PUMPS

AS MENTIONED IN THIS NARRATIVE, we had a gray CJ5 Jeep with a canvas top and a plow on front that could be removed after the winter season passed. To fuel this vehicle without going to town was a gas tank buried underground right in front of the paint shed. Located over the top of this tank was a concrete pad with a hand pump. The pump was a centrifugal device with a handle which was turned in a circular motion. As we turned the handle, the pump would create a vacuum and push the gasoline up from the tank below to the fill the vehicle's gas tank. I can't remember how many turns of the handle per gallon, but it was a lot of work turning the handle enough times to fill the vehicle's tank. The gasoline was purchased and delivered by the same company that had the contract for the heating oil. Shorty was the oil deliveryman who filled the tanks during my time at Split Rock.

THE PAINT SHED

WHEN WALKING DOWN THE ASPHALT ROADWAY between the houses and garages, straight ahead east was the paint shed and gas pumps. The paint shed was a poured concrete building that ran north and south, with the door on the south side, facing the light tower. Inside the building was a rack of shelves on the right or east side. We stored all of the paint, thinner, brushes, rollers, ladders, and whatever used around the station for upkeep and maintenance. A bunch of old stuff that no one ever threw away also found its way into this building. I do recall an old megaphone like the ones cheerleaders use today. Held up to the mouth it amplified the voice. I think it was used to hail ships, boats, and boaters years ago. I don't recall any thing else in there; it was just old stuff. When Split Rock closed permanently, we were told to throw all the old stuff in the dump, so we hauled more than one trailer full there. We just thought it was old junk and had no idea that the lighthouse would be restored in the future.

THE INSIDE OF THE BURNED GARAGE BEFORE IT BURNED
December 1968

THERE WERE THREE GARAGES AT THE STATION, one for each residence, The third garage was our workshop. It was also our daily meeting place to start the workday. Whoever was the officer in charge at the station would come up with the daily work plan and share his ideas with me as to what was to be done at the station that day. He and I were the whole work crew. Len Woodard was one who would do his share of what ever physical job that needed to be done. Bruce Robb was more of a delegater, he'd tell me what needed to be done and then he'd let me do it. He was more interested in being the boss and officer in charge that being a worker. Jim Schubert was a hands-on guy like Len and would pitch right in and do what needed to be done.

For the most part, I didn't care if I did the work or he did it or we did it. It needed to be done, so it got done. We lived where we worked and didn't have to go anywhere, had alternating nights and weekend duty which was a whole lot better than being on search and rescue with a fifteen minute recall. Being stationed and working at Split Rock was so much better than being in Duluth and as a married man with a family, I didn't mind at all.

We would come out of our houses and meet in the third garage each weekday morning. If the officer in charge didn't come out before 8:30, it meant he wasn't going to work that day, and I could tackle any work project that I wanted. Whatever season we were in dictated what needed to be done. The uniform of the day was always dungarees, a chambray shirt, and black work shoes and usually no hat in the summer and a stocking/watch cap with a foul weather jacket in the winter. I wore a pair of sorrel snow packs with steel toes and felt inner liner for a winter work boot

The main door into the garage was of the sliding variety and it faced the light tower to the south. Inside the work garage, a sixteen-foot overheard door was to the left and the stairs to the upstairs apartment was to the right. The apartment was used by single Coastguardsman who helped operate the lighthouse and fog signal in the summer and was at the station as seasonal help. Directly across from the sliding door to the north was the work bench, and behind it on the wall was a peg board with all the hand tools used around the station on a frequent basis. To the right of the work bench, on the east wall under the stairway, was a window. In front of the window was a table that held what ever was being torn apart and fixed that day or week. To the left of the work bench was the two-pot gravity oil burner that was responsible for the fiery destruction of the work garage in the middle of the winter in 1968-1969. To the left of the oil burner was the Jari sickle bar mower/snow blower.

Going out of the garage to the west though the big door and straight ahead was the no-longer-used pump house. To the right of the of the pump house was the vehicle repair ramp. This ramp was a homemade affair constructed out of railroad ties with two thick planks parallel to each other and spaced apart far enough so a person could drive a vehicle onto it. As the ground dropped away, we could crawl under the vehicle to change oil, adjust brakes, and fix exhaust systems and any other vehicle repair that might be needed. I don't know who built it as it was there when I got to Split Rock. Woodard and I never talked about it, it was just there and we used it whenever we needed. it

We changed the oil in the C-J-5 Jeep when the weather was nice out. Len was always doing something on vehicles. He was a bit of a motor head and mechanic. The other two officers in charge, not so much. Robb wasn't interested, and Schubert was not there long enough and it was winter during his short tenure. I used the ramp from time to time to fix the Pontiac when things went wrong on it, and, as it got older, that was quite often.

The ceiling was open floor joists with cross braces. The garage did not have an automatic door opener, so we had to pull it up by hand. The floor was wooden with strong planks that did not bow or bend when we drove the vehicles inside for repair. We kept the Jeep in the garage most of the time. When we used it as a workshop and needed the room, we'd park the Jeep on the repair ramp outside so it was out of the way. With the oil burner going, we could work in our shirtsleeves as it was nice and warm. It had a circulating fan that moved the hot air around. At about 3:00 or 4:00 P.M., we would stop work for the day and turn the oil heater down. In the morning, the first guy in to work would turn it back up, and the shop got nice and warm again.

Out behind the garage on the north side, Len and I built a wooden stand for an oil tank. The tank was about three feet in diameter and about eight to ten feet long. In it, we stored the #1 fuel oil that fed the oil burner in the garage. When the garage burned down, the oil level in the tank was about three-quarters full and the stand it was resting in didn't burn up. We were just lucky the tank didn't start on fire too. After the fire, the garage structure was burned right to the ground with nothing standing except the oil tank. Jim Schubert's new car was burned beyond recognition—you couldn't tell what kind of car it was or if it was old or new. It was burned to a crisp.

REFUGE IN THE UPSTAIRS OF OUR GARAGE
Summer 1967, 1968

WHILE LIVING AT SPLIT ROCK, there were times when everywhere we looked, there were people either staring at us or asking yet another question about the lighthouse. At times, Mark would be crying or Mary needed something done, and it was difficult to find a place to just be me. I didn't always want to be the lighthouse keeper with the answers to all of the lighthouse questions, the worker who was ready to fix anything broken or needed attention, or the father who was always there. Sometimes I just need to be a guy who just wanted to be by himself for a while for a little quiet time in a place of tranquility. It was not that I was so busy, busy, busy, or that I even wanted to be a hermit, but I just needed a get-away place where no one knew where I was every minute of the day, all day long. I found it up in the loft of our garage.

The residence and garages at Split Rock Lighthouse looking east. February 1968. (Photo Mike Roberts)

The stairway, on the east end of the building, lead to peace and quiet, my loft of refuge, a place to get away from it all, to read or just be. It was an unfinished space with bare rafters and roof boards overhead. On windy days, I could hear the wind whistling through the cracks around the doors. The only furniture up there was a comfortable old over-stuffed green chair that some nameless resident had left behind years ago and an orange crate for a book shelf. I would go to the library in Silver Bay and check out books on national, state and local North Shore history, do it yourself projects, autobiographies and self-help. I didn't buy them, just read and brought them back when finished. I also found that the Reader Digest Condensed books had great stories of fiction or non-fiction in them but I couldn't recall where they came from.

The loft was unheated, so during the late spring, summer, and early fall was when my get away spot was used the most. There was a window in the east wall gable of the garage that had a resident spider. It would spin its intricate web to catch unsuspecting insects attracted to the daylight coming through the window, as they were looking for an escape route to the outside. I don't remember any mice running around as there was nothing for them to eat. It was a great spot of solitude, a place to sit and let the world go by and contemplate my family's future.

CHAPTER EIGHT

PASTIMES AT SPLIT ROCK

GOING OUT TO GET THE MAIL

ON HIGHWAY 61, THE LIGHTHOUSE had a mailbox on the lake side or east side of the road, across from the Admunson's home. It was a large galvanized box mounted on a break-away post. If a vehicle or the snow plow hit it, the box on the post would swing around and not be destroyed. The distance from the lighthouse to the mailbox was about half a mile. Mary and I would walk out to get the mail, and sometimes I would take Terry and Cheryl for the mail walk. The road was paved with asphalt/tar with gravel shoulders. In the gravel shoulders were bits and pieces of agates that were naturally occurring in the local pits. I showed the Woodard kids how to find agates using the sun. As agate seekers walked along , they should have the sun shining in their faces. The sun shone through the agates, making them easy to spot on the ground. The trick was not to look at the rocks intently but to look for the sun shining through the translucent stones. They stuck out as little beacons from the ground. Mary and I always looked for agates whenever we could. We would put the small agates we found on the gravel base of the tower so the kids could find them as they played up there. A few of the visitors found them too, not knowing that they were planted for the Woodard kids.

GOING SHOPPING IN DULUTH FOR GROCERIES,
December 1966 to February 1969

GOING SHOPPING DULUTH WAS an all-day affair. We'd go down there about mid-morning and stay until late afternoon or early evening and then head back up the shore to Split Rock and home. One of our favorite shopping places was the Goodwill Store, where we would go bargain hunting to our hearts' delight. Everything we bought was used but still in good shape, and, with little haggling, we might be able to afford whatever we thought we needed at the time.

I was fascinated by the floor set toilet with the flush tank elevated about six feet above the floor. It had a long two-inch flush tube so when the toilet was flushed, it had so much siphonic flushing action that anything within reason was sewer bound. The pull chain connected to the flush handle ran down to the floor to accommodate all sizes of users, and the flushing sound was very distinctive, unlike the toilets of today.

We bought a small wooden rocker for our son Mark, and it was his own special chair for many years until he grew out of it. We also bought a wooden porch swing, that after refinishing, we hung on the front porch facing the lake of our Split Rock home and spent many hours swinging and planning our future on warm summer days

At lunch time, we would stop at Henry's Hamburgers on London Road/Highway 61 and splurge on a couple of fast-food hamburgers. Mark, when he was just a little guy, learned how to drink through a straw at Henry's, and we were so proud of his accomplishment. Later, Henry's became Sandy's which became Hardies, and then I think it was demolished when they brought I-35 to London Road. We have great memories of that place.

Toward the end of the day, we would go up the hill on Central Entrance to the Duluth Air Force Base Commissary to do our monthly or bi-weekly shopping. When coming through the gate, there was an armed air policeman guarding the entrance to the base. He would stop the car and ask where we were going and why. After getting all the right answers, he would smartly wave us through to go and do our shopping. The commissary was a modern supermarket just for military personnel, and their dependants. It was set up just like any store anywhere except the prices on everything were much cheaper. I don't think Uncle Sam made much of a profit on the merchandise in the store. This was a perk for the underpaid service member. They had every thing from soup to nuts including meat, milk, canned everything and bakery goods. We would stock up on as much as our money could buy. We had a freezer at Split Rock so we even bought milk and froze it to take advantage of the cost savings at the government store.

We would heap our shopping cart with our selections and take them to the check-out counter. The cashier demanded my military ID before she would start to ring up your purchases. No ID, no purchasing. There were no UPC information back in those days as the scanner hadn't been invented as of yet, so it seemed like it took forever to go through the line as they entered in each item code by hand.

After ringing everything up, the cashier would pass the purchase to a bag boy and he'd bag it up for us. When I say bag boy, I'm stretching the term "boy" as most of them were old guys in their sixties and seventies. They only worked for tips, so when they bagged our groceries and carried them out to our car, the red 1961 Pontiac wagon, they were doing it as a courtesy because what little money we had left over we were not going to give it to an old guy who the bag boy. I felt funny stiffing the old guys, but I could have bagged our own stuff and hauled it to our car ourselves. We didn't ask for their help. They helped us because it was their job. When they went on their break, they probably talked about that cheap Coast Guard guy from Split Rock who didn't tip them. When leaving the base, we'd go right home as we had frozen foods and perishable meat. We couldn't afford to lose any of it, as it would be about a month or so before we'd go back to shop.

Highway 61 from Duluth near the Lester River, up to Two Harbors was a four-lane, divided, modern freeway. It was a limited-access highway that had a few cross roads but for the most part was pretty straight and recently built. Going north past Two Harbors on 61 was a different matter. The road was twisty and turny with very few places to pass. The road around Silver Creek was very high and scary, there was a sharp turn along the cliff face. We slowed down and were very cautious on that stretch of road, especially when there was snow and ice during the winter. I recall a horror story of three guys who went sailing off the edge of Silver Cliff to their doom in the 1950s. They worked on the construction of Silver Bay or Taconite Harbor when they were being built. We made sure that that did not happen to us.

In the summer the road from Two Harbors to Split Rock was very busy, it was an ordeal to follow all the gawking tourists who traveled along the North Shore. Going slow as not to miss the beautiful scenery was what they came up the North Shore to do. Most of them got their money's worth to the detriment of the local people as we followed in a line of eight to ten vehicles poking along at a snails pace. After all, we had seen these sights hundreds of time before and just wanted to get home. But the summer season was backed up traffic caused by the touring visitors and we had to be extra careful when we got to Gooseberry Falls, so we didn't run anyone down. They'd cross the road on the bridge there with out looking all of the time. Kids were downright scary. If I was in their shoes, maybe I'd get caught up in Nature and do the same thing.

The road had very few places where passing was possible, so when we got to a passing place, we'd have to gun it to get past all of the sightseers before we ran out of room and would have to wait for the next clear spot to pass. Sometimes we'd get caught up in the beauty right along with the tourists and realize just how lucky we were. The scenery was fabulous.

After reaching home, we'd unload the month's provisions into the pantry off the kitchen and freeze the extra milk, meat, and bread. As we thawed the milk, we'd have to be on top of how fast we drank it, as microwave ovens were not available to the consuming public as of yet. We'd thaw it out by putting it in the refrigerator and letting it stand for a few days. We saved all of the milk cartons and rinsed them out and used them to freeze smelt that we caught during the springtime smelt run. Going shopping in Duluth was the highlight of our month, and we looked forward to it, no matter what the season.

GOING TO FINLAND FOR GROCERIES
December 1966 to February 1969

As a member of the Armed Services, I had some privileges that civilians did not have. One of these privileges was shopping at the Military Commissary and the PX. From Split Rock the nearest commissary was the Finland Radar Station. An identification card was issued to each service member which was valid at any military installation anywhere in the United States. With the ID card came the guarantee of admission to any Post Exchange or Base Exchange, which is not the same as the commissary. The PX or BX is more like a department/drug store and the commissary is like a grocery store. When going to the commissary in Finland, the choices were limited, but the prices much lower than the off-base prices in Silver Bay or Two Harbors stores.

Due to the fact that I didn't make very much money in the Coast Guard, we tried to shop at the commissary as much as possible to conserve our meager money supply.

The Finland Radar Station was on top of the hill a little north of the town, was quite small, and not many people were stationed there. Bread, milk, meat, and soap had somewhat less variety at the commissary there, so we bought up for our immediate needs, but saved up our big shopping when we went to Duluth. At Finland, all of the meat was already frozen, so we couldn't really see or smell what we were getting. The only real good deal was on cigarettes at $2. 00 a carton with a limit of two cartons per visit. Many people wanted us to buy them smokes as that price was so cheap in those days. Being a smoker at the time, I consumed all my allotment. If I tried to purchase more, they would give me a hassle, which might result in losing my purchasing privileges. We stuck with buying two cartons at a time with no hassle.

MAKING PICNIC TABLES AND SIGNS
Summer 1968

OUR SPLIT ROCK GARAGE WAS DIRECTLY ACROSS the asphalt roadway to the north of our house, which was the last house to the west. The garage usually housed our car, especially in the winter, but in the summer when it was nice, it became my carpenter shop. Bill Wegner, my stepfather, asked me if I would build some picnic tables and make a big wooden sign for his campground at Garden Lake, which was short distance from the rural town of Section 39 near Ely. Garden lake was located a couple of miles down the road on the other side of the Silver Rapids Bridge on the north end of White Iron Lake. I asked Bill how big he wanted them and how many? After we settled on how big , how many, and who would pay for what, I got a pattern of what he wanted and was excited to go to work.

I bought the wood from a lumberyard right across from Flood Bay on Highway 61 a mile or so north from two Harbors. The husband and wife who owned the place

Mary, Mark, and Mike Roberts sitting on a picnic table at their Split Rock home. (Photo Mike Roberts)

were very nice people. There wasn't any pressure-treated wood as of yet in the 1960s, so to preserve it, it was coasted with a wood preservative that was greenish clear in color. I painted all of the picnic pieces with this preservative before I started to cut out the pieces. I made a few patterns out of wood and traced these patterns on the two-by-four that would be come the tables. I cut all of the wood to length, drilled the holes in the right places and assembled them with screws, nuts, and bolts. I numbered each piece before disassembly then was able to reassemble them without any problem, just by matching up the numbers. Voila! A finished picnic table. I hauled the pieces to Ely in my two-wheeled trailer, and it went well.

I worked on making these tables after the day's work was done. I usually closed the garage doors because the tourists would stop by and want to talk about the lighthouse. I was okay with talking with people, but I also wanted to get the tables done, so I would close the doors so as not to be rude to keep working. It's pretty hard to talk over a operating circular saw. If I left the door open, the sound of the saw drew people in, and I never got anything done except to talk to the visitors. Even with the doors closed, sometimes people would open them up and walk right in while I was working to ask the same old questions. I really didn't mind too much, but it was hard

Seaman Mike Roberts standing in the doorway of their Split Rock home. Note the sign on the fence and the flowers on the porch ledges. (Photo Mary Roberts)

to get much done when I was interrupted all of the time. I made many picnic tables at Split Rock and at times wondered if the preservatives on them really did any good.

I was also asked by my parents to make a six-by-eight wooden sign with the campground logo on it to be placed at the entrance. I did have the a router, bits, and the time to do it. So I said I'd give it a try. I never made a big sign before but had made small wooden signs for Woodard and myself to put out in front of quarters. We hung them on the fence and they looked pretty good too. I think I still have the one I made for our house. Lee Radzak found it years back and sent it to me. A big sign would be a lot bigger challenge that a small sign.

I asked my folks just what was it they were looking for and they showed me one of their business card with a picture of a guy crouched down by a campfire with a tent in the background. It was a great business card but how to make a large sign was another matter. Remembering how I made the Disney Character on Mark's wall, I followed the same basic steps. I traced the picture from the business card on to some onion skin paper and put it into a blank slide frame coated it with vegetable oil to make it transparent and with a slide projector projected it on the six-by-eight sign blank. The sign was assembled in two pieces so I could haul it in the car and then reassemble it again. I traced the picture on to the sign blank and then routed out the outline of the picture. I spray painted the routed-out part with green paint, and when it got dry, sanded all the over spray off. The sign looked great. My folks were pleased and put it up at the entrance to the campground. It looked very professional, and I took great pride in how it came out.

The picnic tables and sign were used for many years and were probably sold at the break up of the campground when the land was converted into residences, years ago or ended up on someone's burn pile and used for firewood.

PICKING AGATES & THE ROCK TUMBLER
Summer 1967 and 1968

THE NORTH SHORE OF LAKE SUPERIOR is a treasure trove of agates. They are found on the beaches, gravel roads, and gravel pits. People looking for them should always walk toward the sun on a sunny day . That way they can be seen shining as they lay waiting to de discovered. Mary and I had little money when we were in the service so we had to make our own inexpensive fun. We picked agates. Before our kids started to come along, we could pick up and go agate hunting whenever we had time. At Split Rock, I worked from 8:00 to 5:00 daily and had alternating duty weekends. On duty weekends, I didn't have to work except turn the light on and off at the correct time. I also just had to be there so the visitors wouldn't tear the place up. It was the presence of Coast Guard personnel on the site that indicated to everyone that it was a working lighthouse.

After our Mark was born, we still wanted to pick rocks, but he was too heavy to carry, and the baby backpacks were very expensive. Mary and I formulated a plan. We would go over to Highway 3 that ran through the backwoods between Two Harbors and Finland. It was still gravel in those days. We would put Mark in our 1961 Pontiac station wagon sleeping in a car bed just for babies. I would drop Mary off and drive up the road about 100 yards or so. After checking to make sure our baby was happy and sleeping, I parked the car on the shoulder of the road. Then I'd get out and start walking up the gravel road looking for agates as I went.

Mary was walking up the road looking for agates would eventually get up to our parked car. She'd check on our baby, start the car and drive it past me going up the road about another 100 yards and park on the shoulder, check the baby, get out and start walking up the road on the hunt for agates. I would walk up to where the car was parked after looking for agates all the way, get in, check on our baby and drive past Mary. In this way were able to leap frog up the road, watch our baby and pick agates too. It never occurred to us that something might go wrong, and it never did. We found many beautiful if small stones, some of which we made into jewelry.

My folks, Clarence "Bill" and Helen Wegner were rock hounds from way back. They belonged to the Mesabi Rock & Mineral Club. When I was a young kid in high school, we would go to the North Shore from Ely, look for agates and make a whole day out of it. I'd take my friend Barry Williams along with us, and we'd pack a picnic lunch, leave early in the morning, look for rocks, see all of the sights and stay all day. We would come home after dark, tired but had lots of stories to tell about the day's happenings.

Bill had a three-barrel rock tumbler he used to tumble agates. The barrels were rubber lined and had a removable leak proof cover. In the first barrel he put rough agates with some heavy grit and water. In the next barrel, a medium grit and water was put in the second barrel with agates that came out of the first barrel. The third barrel was for the agates after they came out of the second barrel. The stones had to be washed carefully of all grit before going into the third barrel. Jewelers' rouge was mixed with the water and placed in that last barrel to give the rocks a polished sheen that made them sparkle. The polishing took about three months from start to finish.

Bill loaned us the tumbler, and we had it under the steps down in the basement right next to the home-brewed beer. When we closed the under-the-steps closet door, we couldn't hear the constant sound of the rotating tumbler and the stones against each other in the rest of the house. The Coast Guard supplied us electricity, Bill gave us the tumbler and the grits for it, so it didn't cost us any thing to tumble agates to a fine polish.

After the third barrel was finished, we'd make jewelry from the polished stones. When we had some finished pieces, we brought them over to the Split Rock gift shop next door. Mr. and Mrs. Francis, the owners, would sell it for us, take a small cut for their time and shelf space and give us the rest. We didn't get rich. We barely broke even with the cost of the glue and findings even with the tumbling process being free, but it gave us something to do, got us out of the house for a little while, and it was fun, too.

Bill Wegner made a water wheel to polish agates without using electricity. He put it in the Shagawa River downstream from Winton. The undershot water wheel rotated in the river for many years as it turned rough agates into polished stones.

SMOKED FISH
Summers of 1967 and 1968

WHILE STATIONED AT SPLIT ROCK, I had a lot of time to do many things, one of which was smoking fish. It was an old tradition of the North Shore and thought by some to be a delicacy. I found an old refrigerator in the Beaver Bay dump and brought it home to Split Rock. When I told Mary what I was planning to do with it, she thought I was nuts. I made a small cuts in the door gasket of the refrigerator in each corner, top and bottom to let a little air into the smoker. Next, I screwed two two-by-fours about three-quarters of the way up from the bottom on either side of the door to hold the fish racks. I cut two other two-by-fours to length to sit on top of the wood on the side of the refrigerator. Into these two-by-fours, which ran the width of the smoker, I drove some nails on both sides about three inches apart at an angle so the points were sticking up. On these nails, the fish would be impaled through the back of their head and would hang with their tails down.

I got an old electric hot plate from the Goodwill store down in West Duluth. I think I paid a couple of bucks for the hot plate and an old cast iron frying pan. Next, I got some green alder brush from a nearby swamp to use as a source of smoke. I'd also use apple wood when I could find some. I put the hot plate, set on low, into the bottom of the smoker and put the frying pan full of green alder on the top of the burner. When I closed the refrigerator (now smoker) door, it would start to smoke after a while. The limited air supply would enter on the bottom where I cut the gasket away, and the smoke eventually escaped through the top of the door where the gasket cuts were.

Everything was ready. All I needed was some fish. The Mattsons in East Beaver Bay had a fish store at the time. They sold fresh and smoked fish. However, this fish was way too expensive for us. There were two Mattson brothers, both commercial fishermen who had a fish house and dock on the lake shore just down the hill from the store. They only fished a couple of days a week, so I had to see them when they came in off the lake. I asked at the fish store, and they told me when the brothers came in with their catch.

I went down to see them, told them that I was in the Coast Guard stationed at Split Rock and would they sell me some fish right off of their boat? They said sure, but they'd have to get fifteen cents a pound for it and had to take the gills out before they could sell them. They told me they checked the gills for some kind of fish disease. If they found it, they had to report it to the State Fisheries Department. I said I'd like about twenty to thirty pounds of fish, and they said okay.

After they gutted, gilled, and weighed the herring and sisco, they put a bunch in a wash tub I had brought along for that purpose. They gave me way more than I wanted and hardly charged me anything.

They sold some of their fish in the store, but most of it was gilled, gutted, split in half, salted and put into wooden kegs and sold as salt herring. They said it was exported to Scandinavia, where they got a good price for it. . . . They also said they were happy that the Coast Guard was still running the lighthouse and would come looking for them if they ever got in trouble out on the lake. Get in trouble they did, years later. I heard that those same Mattson brothers fell overboard from their boat and drowned. Found in their own nets, or so the story goes. It's a shame. They were really nice guys. Lake Superior is mighty cold all year around. When I see people in small boats out on the lake, I think they're taking their lives in their hands. I think they're nuts. One mistake, one stupid move, and a person can be dead—even good swimmers—because the risk on Lake Superior isn't only the drowning but the hypothermia of that icy water.

After I brought the fish home, I washed them out and split open the tail below the anus so the salt brine could get inside the tail meat. I got some softener salt and made a very strong brine to soak the fish in overnight. The next day I rinsed them off with a garden hose and put them on the nails of the long two-by-fours and hung them in the smoker. Then I turned the hot plate on low and went about my daily chores around the lighthouse. I'd check the progress from time to time throughout the day to see how the fish was doing. Late in the day, after about eight or ten hours of smoking, I'd shut the smoker off and let it cool down before taking out the fish. Sometimes as I would be taking the fish out of the smoker, tourists visiting the lighthouse would want to know if the smoked fish was for sale. We usually had more than we could eat, so I sold some. But we really liked the results and ate most of the fish ourselves. We would also bring some over to Ely. My stepfather, Bill Wegner, loved smoked fish.

SAUSAGE MAKING, ALL THE
WHILE LIVING AT SPLIT ROCK

THE HUNGARIANS MAKE A WONDERFUL SAUSAGE called Kolbasz. It's coarse ground pork, garlic, paprika, and other spices mixed and stuffed into casings. When Mary was a growing up, her family ate it a lot. Her Uncle Paul Lakatas use to make it at home and then sell it to all the relatives to cover his costs. I acquired a taste for it, and it wasn't too expensive to make, so we added Kolbasz to our Split Rock diet. The ingredients were mixed together, stuffed into casings, which were the small intestines of pigs or the manufactured equivalents. We did not have a sausage stuffer, so I had to make one out of steel pipe. The pipe was about twenty-four inches long with threads on both ends. On one end was a pipe cap with a hole drilled in the center.

A three-eighths-inch nut was brazed on the cap over the center of the hole. A three-eighths threaded rod was screwed into the nut. I turned two wooden wheels out of three-quarter-inch wood that were just a little smaller than the inside bore of the pipe. A seven-sixteenths-inch hole was drilled dead center of the two wheels just large enough to let the three-eighths-inch rod pass through it. I cut a piece of leather just big enough to stick out all around the two wheels and sandwiched the leather between the two wheels. The leather was the scraper/plunger that would make a seal between the plunger and the side walls of the pipe. The plunger pushed the meat out of the stuffer into the casings. I double nutted the three-eighths-inch rod on either side of the wood and leather plunger. The rod then was threaded through the nut on the two-inch cap.

On the other end of the two-inch pipe, a two-by-three-quarters-inch galvanized reducing coupling was threaded on the pipe. Into the three-quarter-inch end of the fitting, a four-inch galvanized pipe nipple was screwed to hold the casing as it was being stuffed. With the reducing coupling screwed on one end of the pipe, the meat was loaded into the barrel of the stuffer. The cap, plunger, and rod were screwed on to the end of the barrel. With an electric drill, the end of the rod was tightened into the chuck of an electric drill. When the trigger was pulled, the drill turned the rod, which pushed the plunger against the meat and forced it out the other end into the sausage casings.

I had the barrel in a vice but a garage bench is not particularly sanitary. So, I made an assembly out of two two-by-fours about eighteen inches long and hinged them together on one end. I drilled a hole in the two-by-fours on the opposite end of the hinges and put a nut and bolt through the hole and tightened it up to clamp on the barrel and held it tightly. After a few refinements of the two-by-four clamps on the barrel, I got it so the stuffer could be assembled and disassembled without too much trouble. This assembly I could use, then clean and store. This stuffer came under the heading of "necessity is the mother of invention." We used it for many years, but it got lost in one of our many moves.

Smelt fishing
Spring of 1967 and 1968

Mary and I had very little money at Split Rock, so we did many things to entertain ourselves, make some money if we could and try to save what little money we did have. A money-saving activity which we did in the spring was smelting. In the middle 1960s, the smelt would run up most of the local creeks and rivers including the Split Rock River down Highway 61 a few miles from the lighthouse. When smelting season got under way, usually in the latter part of April, I'd get hold of Bruce Robb and some of my old high school friends living and working in Silver Bay, and we'd go smelting. They'd bring a pint of peppermint schnapps, we'd build a fire down on the beach, talk smart and have fun while we pulled in the fish. What smelting was, for those who never experienced it, was fishing with fine mesh dip nets or seines.

The smelt would run up the stream so thick we could feel them hitting our legs as we waded in with our nets. They would run in big schools as they all tried to come in from the lake at the same time. While smelting, there were periods with a lot of activity, and then times of no activity at all. It was an annual rite of springtime, and people would come from all over for smelting. It was a party atmosphere, kind of a tailgate party on the streams. Everyone had a good time. Sometimes people had just a little too much fun, forgetting the danger of the ice-cold streams in the springtime and would drown.

One year, a mink farmer from North Dakota came to smelt with a dump truck and garbage cans. It was just him and his son. The going was kind of slow for them as they filled their garbage cans with fish and hauled them back up the hill to their truck parked on the side of the road. It was heavy, tedious work, but the fish were free food for their mink, and the smelt just kept coming in.

We took some heavy-weight garbage bags and filled them up many of them and hauled them up to their truck so they could take the fish home and freeze them for mink food. It didn't take very long as there were lots of guys helping, and the fish were really running heavy that particular night. Dennis Koschak and Bernie Zupancich were a couple of Ely guys I remember who lent a hand to those Dakota mink farmers.

At other times, I would go net the smelt alone and bring home a washtub full. Mary and I would clean them with scissors by the thousands. We saved all of our empty milk cartons all year long, fill them with the cleaned smelt, add salt water and freeze them in our government-provided deep freezer. We ate smelt at least once a week sometimes more, all year round. I still love smelt to this day.

Sometimes I'd go down where everyone was smelting and ask to could pick some really big ones out of their catch. They usually had so many that they gave me all I could haul. I'd take them home, gut them, leave the heads on and smoke them. Smelt smoked with green alder and apple wood are just delicious. I haven't had any since we left Split Rock.

Making Beer
Fall and Winter 1968

We burned fuel oil in the boiler that heated the houses, so from time to time we needed a fuel oil delivery. A guy named Shorty was the fuel truck driver delivery man. He was a friendly guy who loved to talk as he worked, and not being a shy or retiring guy myself, we had many great conversation during his fuel trips to Split Rock. During one such delivery, he was telling me about the beer he was making and how great it was. That piqued my interest, so I asked him for the recipe for his home brew. I have included it here for all the home-brewed beer enthusiasts who read this. I take no responsibility for the results, but it worked well for me.

Fill a ten-gallon crock or container half full of lukewarm water (about five gallons) and mix in a cake of yeast. Add seven pound of sugar and one can of Blue Ribbon Malt. Mix this up thoroughly. Fill the rest of the container with water to make ten gallons. Cover the container with a cloth and let it stand until you don't see any more bubbles coming up from the bottom. If it isn't warm enough, put a trouble light under it for the heat. It should be about seventy to seventy-five degrees. It should take about about three days before it can be bottled. Put a teaspoonful of sugar in the bottom of each bottle before you fill the bottles. Cap the bottles or seal with wax if you don't have a bottle capper. Store the capped bottles in a dark room for ten to twelve days before you drink it.

We pumped the water for the station out of the lake and added chlorine to kill any bacteria. I didn't think that our water would make very good beer. We went to the London Crossing Spring on the old Two Harbors to Finland road to get spring water for the brew. According to the locals, the London Crossing spring was a watering stop for horses as people traveled up the North Shore. The pipe came directly out of the hillside, and the water was so cold that it hurt my teeth. It had no turbidity and was delicious, just right for making home brewed beer. I had gotten some five-gallon galvanized cans with tops from Mr. Francis, who used them when he had to haul water to his gift shop years ago.

Mary and I loaded the cans into the Pontiac wagon and took off for the spring. We filled them to the brim and put the tops on the cans to stop them from sloshing out and brought them home for our home-brew adventure. We mixed up all of the ingredients just like Shorty's recipe called for and watched to see when the bubbles stopped rising to the top. We siphoned the liquid into the bottles after adding the sugar to each bottle and capped and sealed them in wax. We stored the bottles in the closet under the steps and let them age for twenty-eight days.

When the aging was over, we took one bottle out. It had turned a lovely amber color and looked just like beer. We unscrewed the top and sniffed. It smelled like beer, and, to our pleasure, after taking a little sip, we knew it tasted like beer. By George, it *was* beer. Problem was, it packed a wallop that made us tipsy after a few pulls on the bottle. On the bottom of the bottle was a white residue called "mother." The first few bottles we were careful not to include the mother in the beer glass but after a few beers, you really didn't care if you drank the bottom or not.

It was good stuff if you were a serious beer drinker.

PICKING SCRAP METAL AND POP BOTTLES

I PAID MORE MONEY IN INCOME TAXES in 1966 than I made in 1967, not that we lived high on the hog or anything before going into the service, but it was quite a financial come down to be in Uncle Sam's military service and a member of the United States Coast Guard. However, being broke was much better than being in combat where you would be in danger and still broke.

Mary and I were always looking for ways to augment our income, to bring in just a little more cash to tide us over. One day, as I was walking out to get the mail, I spied some pop bottles in the ditch, thrown there by some litterbug tourist. I picked them up and brought them home as there was a two-cent per bottle refund. The bottling companies would take them back and reuse them, unlike today where most things are thrown away. Only the major brands like Coca Cola, Pepsi, Orange Crush, Hires Root Beer, 7-Up, and the like were redeemable. We'd collect all the bottles we could find that weren't broken and turn them in for a little bit of money. It wasn't much, but it was something. The bottles with the twist-off caps weren't redeemable, but we could use them for bottling home-brew beer and wine, so we saved them too. We had fun looking for them, kind of like a treasure hunt. We didn't go rummaging through garbage cans or dumpsters though. We just looked along the roadsides near Split Rock.

While we were hunting for bottles, we also looked for scrap steel, brass, and copper. The Vietnam War was going hot and heavy and the price of scrap copper was worth our while to pick it up and save for resale. I would build a bonfire over by the hoist house and burn the covering off of any copper wire we found as they wanted clean scrap. In those days, it wasn't illegal to burn trash or anything for that matter. I'd burn the paper refuse from our living quarters at the same time as I burned the copper. After accumulating scrap metal for some time and separating it into like piles, we would put it into grocery bags, load them in to our car and, on our way to going shopping at the Air Force Base, take it to the scrap yard in Duluth. The junk man would weigh each pile of metal and pay us accordingly. It wasn't very much cash for our efforts, but when you have very little money, even a little extra was most appreciated.

CHAPTER NINE

DRIVING AROUND SPLIT ROCK

THE BURNED OUT CLUTCH
Winter 1966-1967

LEN AND DORIS WOODARD LEFT before Christmas to go home to North Carolina and spend the holidays with their families. They would usually take a thirty-day leave for their annual visit. The lighthouse light was shut off as the shipping season was finished and wouldn't come back on until spring, but because it was our home as well as duty station, Mary and I would keep the home fires burning, the road plowed and the walks shoveled. The Coast Guard Jeep's clutch was on its last legs as it was a snowy winter and a lot of plowing had been done, wearing it out. I called headquarters at Group Duluth and told them that the clutch was going and wouldn't last much longer. They told me to bring it to a garage down in Two Harbors and have it replaced.

After the repair arrangements were made, I drove the Jeep, down and Mary fol-lowed in the red Pontiac wagon. The garage said it would take a couple of days to get the clutch replaced and to come back when it was done to pick it up. We went back to Split Rock and hoped it wouldn't snow too much. I called the garage a few days later, and they said it would be done in that afternoon and to come down late in the after-noon to pick it up. Just in time, I might add, as the storm clouds were gathering, and a snow storm was supposed to hit soon. We would need the Jeep to plow the impending snow. It was late in the afternoon when we went to pick the Jeep up, and a few flakes were starting to fall. After getting the Jeep back on the road and heading up the shore, it was getting dark, and those few flakes had turned into a full-blown blizzard. Mary was following close behind the Jeep in the Pontiac.

We couldn't go very fast as the visibility was just about zero. The blowing, drifting snow was fast approaching life threatening, but what could we do? We were on the road and couldn't think of turning back. We didn't know anyone in Two Harbors to stay with anyway, so we thought it best to push on through the blizzard to Split Rock and home.

Mary was not an adventuresome driver and liked her driving conditions dry and in daylight as her night eyes weren't the best, but she hung in there as we traveled Highway 61 northward. As we slowly picked our way, me in the Jeep leading and Mary following close in my tracks, an inconsiderate driver pulled up right behind Mary and proceeded to follow her at about two car lengths away. Their high beams were shining right in her back window and rear view mirror. Hanging on to the steering wheel as tightly as she could, Mary followed the Jeep around the edge of Silver Cliff, full well knowing that at any instant her car would spin out of control and go crashing over the guard rail down to Lake Superior 300 feet below. The moron following Mary didn't let up or back off for one second but trailed behind as if glued to Mary's rear bumper. I, being in the lead, had no idea what was going on behind me and kept picking my way along the shore. I had the Jeep in four-wheel drive so I wouldn't slip and slide around. We finally turned off the main road and spun our way up the hill toward the lighthouse.

It seemed like the usual half-hour-plus drive took hours and hours to reach home and safety. To this day Mary still talks about some of the rotten situations she has been in with me and the clutch repair and homeward blizzard at Split Rock ranks right up there as one of her worst driving experiences, ever.

LEN'S OLD CAR
Summer 1967

LEN WAS FROM NEW BERN, NORTH CAROLINA, and people from that part of the country really liked their cars. Some might even be considered "motor heads." Len was pretty handy and mechanically inclined, so he thought he might buy an old car, fix it up and sell it. Between the second and third garages was our ramp built into the bank so we could change oil or work on the underside of vehicle with out jacking it up or lying on our back. We mostly used it to change our own oil and filters or work on exhaust systems and brakes if need be.

Len bought an old car from a local farmer. It was low on miles and had good glass, but it had been stored for years in the grove of trees. It was all faded out, covered with dirt and grime and was pretty ugly. He brought it home, and Doris asked him what he was going to do with that old piece of junk. He said, "Fix it up and sell it." She had a hard time believing him as the car was really bad looking. He started to clean it up and get it running halfway decently, and I gave him a hand. I didn't have much else to do anyway.

The engine was running rough, so he said he thought the valves were carboned up. After running the engine for a little while to warm it up, he popped open the hood. He had filled a two-quart pop bottle with water from the outside house hydrant. He then removed the air cleaner from the top of the carburetor and, with one hand on the accelerator linkage, raced the engine. With the other hand he started to pour the water slowly right down into the throat of the carburetor. I thought he was nuts and going to ruin the engine. He kept racing the engine and pouring the water until the two-quart bottle was empty.

Out of the exhaust pipe came great billows of rolling steam. It looked like a smoke screen there was so much steam. He ran the engine wide open for a short time and said, "That should do it." I asked, "Do what?" I had never heard, much less seen anyone do that to an engine before. Len explained that carbon could build up on the surface of the valve seats, which would stop the engine from getting good compression. Pouring water though it caused it to steam and blow the carbon out the tail pipe but didn't hurt the engine. I learned a good lesson that day. *It was shut up, watch and listen, you might learn something.* When I learned something, I always store it away, hoping some day to use it before I forgot it.

Flash forward in time to the early 1980s, the place was Jackson, Minnesota, where I had taken a job as a plumbing instructor in a technical college. The students would learn plumbing in the classroom setting and then go out on the job and apply the skills learned in people's houses. We built houses on campus and throughout the town. At times, the class would plumb the new houses of school employees. The employee would furnish the material, and students would supply the labor. It was a win-win arrangement.

We had a couple of old pickups that had seen better days acquired from U.S. Air Force Surplus. The school's mechanics class got them running pretty well, but they were still old beaters without too much life left in them, no matter how one looked at it.

While returning to the school after piping up a house in the country, it was raining hard. The truck I was driving was bucking and trying to stall in the rain storm.

The guy riding shotgun said that it looked like we were getting water in the gas, and I said that I didn't think so, that it felt like it was electrical. He said, "I know cars and engines and I think its water in the gas. "

Knowing what I knew about pouring water down the carburetor during the Split Rock days, again I said I thought it might be electrical. He being a young and impetuous fellow who believed that he could not possibly be wrong, said with more authority, "I know it's water in the gas, and that's all it can be." Not willing to let it go, I said, "That might not be quite true. Water in the gas might cause this reaction, but I'd have to go with an electrical problem." He once again said, "No way."

I was the teacher wasn't I? It was my responsibility to teach the students a lesson they could take with them for the rest of their lives, wasn't it? It didn't necessarily have to be about plumbing; it could be about life in general. So I said to the student who knew he was right beyond a shadow of a doubt, "It's not water in the gas, and to prove it, I'll take a two-liter bottle of water and pour it right down the carburetor, and the engine will not miss a beat but keep running fine. I'll bet you and your buddies that I can do what I say." The students thought that was an absurd idea, that pouring water down the carburetor would certainly kill the engine. They said they would put up. I said that we'd do it after we got on the job tomorrow, but I would run the foot feed, and they should get up as much money as they could afford to lose, and I'd match it. If I lost, I'd pay up, and if they lost, I'd keep their money. They thought I was nuts, just like I thought Len was nuts at Split Rock years before.

When we got to the job site the next day, I had the two-liter bottle of water, and they had expectant grins on their faces, all fifteen of them. The students chipped their $20.00 into a common pot. I put up my money, and we gave it to the guy we were working for to pay out to the winner. The engine was hot, as I slowly opened the hood and took off the air cleaner. I asked the students if they were ready. They all laughed and said they were, that this was going to be the easiest money they ever made.

I revved up the engine with one hand on the linkage and started to pour the water with the other. Not too fast and not too slow. I remembered carefully what Len had done. The water disappeared down the throat of the roaring engine. The students were holding their breaths because they knew that the engine would die and the easy money would be theirs. The engine roared, and the water poured until there was none left in the bottle. Steam was pouring out the exhaust tailpipe at the back of the pickup, huge billows of steam. Just like when Len had done this.

I released the linkage and let the engine idle, walked over to the homeowner holding everyone's money and gently took it from his hand to the stunned silence of the newly educated young guys. I said, "Thank you very much," as I counted out the wad of bills and put it into my pocket. Then as an after thought said, "Oh ya, you can't beat a man at his own game." I had passed on the knowledge of cleaning the carbon out of engine valves that I had learned from Woodard some years before at the Split Rock Lighthouse

SILVER TRAILER
Summer 1967

MARY AND I LIVED IN ELY BEFORE I ENLISTED in the Coast Guard. When my enlistment was up, we were going to go back there to live. We had previously bought, on time, eighty acres of swamp, trees, rocks, and mosquitoes with a log house on it. The house wasn't in too bad of shape, was sound and dry, but had no indoor plumbing or running water, and it needed a lot of work before we could live in it. We thought that we could go back to Ely to fix it up so when we got out of the service—we'd have a place to live.

Before we went into the service, we had a ten-by-fifty Vindale mobile home located on the place, but we had sold it to my folks. They would make the payments on the eighty acres and keep the trailer on the place and rent it out so the vandals wouldn't burn the log house down while we were gone. It wasn't practical to live with my folks when we were working on the house renovation. It would be too hard to balance everyone's schedules. We had a dilemma of where to stay when fixing up the house.

In the spring of 1967, we saw an advertisement in the local paper for the sale of the silver trailers at Taconite Harbor, a docking, loading and power house facility on the North Shore constructed in the early 1950s. It was built by Pickand-Mathers for Erie Mining Company. They mined and processed the taconite ore in Aurora and Hoyt Lakes but needed a place to load up the ships going to the steel mills in Gary, Cleveland, and Detroit.

When the harbor was under construction, they hired many workers. These workers had no place to live, so the company made a temporary town at Taconite Harbor and bought hundreds of small aluminum sided trailers twenty to twenty-five feet long. The trailer had a living room, kitchen, bathroom, and a rear bedroom. The workers rented these from the company for so much a month. They were all the same with an electric stove, refrigerator, and birch paneling throughout. They were nice compact livable homes away from home. When all of the construction on the facility was complete and the company decided to liquidate all of the trailers in the park. In the spring of 1967 we decide to buy one and move it to Ely to take care of our temporary housing needs.

Deciding to buy something was one thing, but paying for it was something else. They wanted a lot of money for one—as I recall it was $500. 00. Mary had worked all of our married life, and when we were transferred to Split Rock, she had to quit her Duluth job. As there were no jobs in the Split Rock area, she collected unemployment in Silver Bay and then graciously donated her unemployment checks to the purchase of the trailer.

We went to look at the trailers, but they sold so fast that there were only a few left, and those needed some work. There was a choice between one with a broken freezer door and an unbroken one. The unbroken one had been spoken for, but there was no money down on it, so I offered the guy who was selling them $20.00 cash for the unbroken one, and he said, okay, it was ours but to get it out of there as quickly as possible.

Now how do we move the trailer? The 1961 Pontiac didn't have a trailer hitch on it, so I couldn't pull it with that. My stepfather, Bill Wegner, had a nephew named Jim (Bizzer) Laberge, who lived in Silver Bay and worked at Reserve Mining Company as a welder. He had a pickup with a hitch on it. I called him up and asked if he would pull the trailer to Split Rock for a tankful of gas and $5.00. He agreed and came to Taconite Harbor, hooked up the trailer and towed it to Split Rock. We parked it on the east side of our garage and proceeded to clean it out and fix it up.

The inside walls were paneled in birch, so we washed them down with Murphy's soap and polished them with Scott's Liquid Gold. I replaced the sink counter top with some good-looking linoleum, and Mary made curtains on her sewing machine. We thought it looked beautiful, and for being as old as it was, it did look cute and wasn't half bad. I washed the outside but couldn't get it to shine as the aluminum was badly oxidized.

We spent many happy hours in the trailer refurbishment and met many nice people who stopped by to comment on it on their way to see the lighthouse. It was parked there for a month or two, and then we again contacted Bizzer Laberge and made arrangement to have it towed to Ely. We kept the trailer, worked on the house, and when it was completed as much as we could do, Jim Bizzer LaBerge again moved it up to Grand Marais for us in the summer of 1969. We rented it out until freeze up to construction workers working on the repavement of Highway 61. We then sold the trailer to a guy from Silver Bay I used to play hockey with. He wanted to use it for a summer cabin on a lake. So, the trailer came in to our life when we need it and left us when its usefulness was complete. I think we made a profit from the rental and sold it for more than we paid for it.

THE TAN 1969 PLYMOUTH WAGON
Late Fall 1968

As I STARTED TO SEARCH FOR ANOTHER CAR and was focusing on a late model used machine preferably a station wagon with low miles in our price range, I read all the want ads in the papers but found nothing suitable as to price and availability. When stopping at a car dealer in Two Harbors, I inquired about a used low-mileage station wagon. The salesman said he didn't have anything right now but to stop back in a week or so and see if something came in we might like and afford. I was getting a little bummed out with the 1961 Pontiac breakdowns as it was nickel and dollaring us to death. I had just replaced the rear axle with one from the junk yard in Superior, Wisconsin. It was getting close to winter, and I didn't want to break down on the road out in the middle of nowhere, with a wife and little baby or when I was on the way to work in Two Harbors.

The salesman asked if I had considered buying a new car. I laughed and said we hardly had enough money for a used one let alone a new one. He said they could stretch the payments out so buying a new one would be just like buying a used one, only it would take longer to pay it off. He showed me what they had in stock and a

The tan 1969 Plymouth station wagon with Eric, age seven, and Tim, age three standing looking at Friskie, our dog in Ely in 1976. (Photo Mike Roberts)

tan 1969 Plymouth station wagon caught my eye. It had a 318 V-8 engine that was easy on gas, four doors to get the kids in and out easily, plenty of room for the kids and a two-way tail gate that opened like a door from the side or pulled down like a tailgate on a pickup truck. My car problems would be solved if we bought the car, but where would we get the money from?

Mary said maybe her grandmother would loan it to us. Mary's grandmother Fodor-Varga was a Hungarian from the old county and a tight wad. She had lots of money that she earned by working for every nickel. The reason she had money was, like most wealthy people, she never spent it on anything unless it could bring her more money to add to her wealth. Mary spent a lot of time with her when she was a little girl, so the woman had a soft spot in her heart for her "sweet little Mary." Mary got in contact with her Grandma and explained our dire car situation. We needed $2,500.00 on a $3,500.00 car and could she loan it to us? Grandma felt sorry for us and sent a check for $2,500.00. Mary borrowed $500.00 from her sister, Marge and by putting those two loans together, we had enough to buy the car with our trade in. Our transportation problems were solved, wheels that would not leave us stranded in the middle of nowhere. We put 150,000 miles on that car. It did everything it was supposed to, and we never had a break down with it. We kept it until the late 1970s when we sold it to a family in Jackson, which was where our home was at the time.

CHAPTER TEN

GRAND MARAIS SEARCH AND RESCUE

THE TOWN OF GRAND MARAIS, MINNESOTA
1969-1970

DURING THE YEARS OF 1969 AND 1970, when we lived there, the town of Grand Marais was struggling to survive. There weren't many major businesses in town, but it was the county seat of Cook County and also the biggest town in the tip of the Minnesota Arrowhead country. There were many well-established resorts up the Gunflint Trail and a few along the lake shore that were supplied by the local stores. The municipal campground was on the west shore of the harbor, directly across from the Coast Guard Life Boat Station. Hedstrom's sawmill, on top of the hill, was a major employer of the townfolk, as was Consolidated paper company. The Forest Service, Coast Guard, and Border Patrol contributed a few people to the town, as did the Northwestern Bell phone company, the post office, and the school system. The town had a municipal on and off liquor store, a couple of grocery stores, numerous churches, a barber shop, a few restaurants, a five and dime/variety store, the hospital, and a few specialty shops that catered to the tourists just passing through. It also had a weekly newspaper, a public library, and a few gas stations.

Someone had a great dream and the foresight to turn the town into a tourist haven/artist colony, and they accomplished that dream. The Grand Marais of today

Grand Marais from on top of Pincushion Hill. (Photo Lila Panek. Used with permission)

Grand Marais Harbor, sheltering sail boats behind the breakwall. (Photo Lila Panek. Used with permission)

is much more vibrant and bustling than the Grand Marais that existed when I was stationed there in 1969 and 1970. There are a lot of people in town and those people bring in money that keeps the town going. It seems to be busy all year round now as opposed to just when summer visitors come or a few skiers at Lutsen and snowmobiling on the Gunflint Trail come in the winter.

THE TRAILER PARK AND
LIVING IN GRAND MARAIS
March 1959 to February 1970

AFTER MARY AND I AND OUR BOYS SETTLED in at Joe Thompson's Trailer Park on the east side of town, we found that even though the mobile home was smaller than our Split Rock home, it was adequate for our short-term living needs in Grand Marais. When spring time finally arrived, we met some of our neighbors, who were very nice. We lived on the western corner of the upper tier of the trailer court and had neighbors on the east side and the bottom tier behind us. The next-door neighbors were the Paneks, Bob and Lila and son, Jason. Bob was a forester for the Bureau of Indian Affairs on the Grand Portage Indian Reservation. He helped them manage their tribal timber lands. Lila was a nurse on the night shift at the local hospital. Mary met her briefly when she had Eric there. Jason became Mark's next door playmate as they were about the same age. When the weather got nice, the snow melted and the frost came out of the ground, Bob and I fenced in the space between our trailers to make a secure playground with a sandbox for our kids so the moms didn't have to watch them every minute of the day. The playground between the trailers worked out well. The kids became friends and played together well by the hour. The rest of the people in our upper tier were very nice as well, all hard-working folks between homes or duty assignments.

Grand Marais was a small isolated town way out in the boonies. Due to the transitory nature of the people serving in the Coast Guard, Border Patrol, and the

Mark Roberts in front of the Roberts's trailer in the trailer court in Grand Marais. (Photo Mike Roberts)

Joe Thompson's trailer court in Grand Marais. (Photo Lila Panek. Used with permission)

Panek's trailer in the trailer court in Grand Marais (Photo Lila Panek. Used with permission)

Forest Service, some of the local people did not welcome us with open arms. I thought this behavior strange. They weren't mean or anything but just kept us at arm's length, a bit stand offish. One would think that because it was a long way from anywhere, the local people would just love to have people from the outside as friends and share their life's experience with them, but that was not the case.

I finally, after a lot of thinking, figured this odd behavior out. Anyone from the Forest Service, Border Patrol, or the Coast Guard who came to town to do their job was a transient, a short-term resident. After their next promotion, they would be leaving for the next assignment, someplace else. It was hard to see friends repeatedly go away and leave them behind. It was easier never became friends in the first place, easier at least on the ones who were left behind in the small town for the rest of their lives. After figuring this out, I knew why the locals chose this survival behavior and that it was not something we, as transients, did to them. The locals and businesses catered to the tourists and summer folk from other places, such as the Twin Cities, Duluth, and Chicago. The tourists brought in the money that kept the town going. This was the norm long before the Grand Marais area became a predominately summer destination of the well-to-do-middle class people who own cottages and summer homes of the present. I wonder if this phenomena of behavior still persists in the town today?

THE DAY ERIC WAS BORN
March 12 1969

WHEN WE CAME TO GRAND MARAIS in March of 1969, Mary was ready to deliver our next child. She didn't have a doctor as of yet, as we just moved to town. I had gone to board up Split Rock Lighthouse with some of the guys from the station, so I wasn't available when the blessed event started to unfold. Mark was a year and a half and not keen on the idea of having his mom being gone for any length of time. Mary called Lil Whalen, the wife of the officer in charge of the station to come and get her to bring her to Dr. McDonald's office, as she didn't have a car. The car was at the station because I had taken it to work that day. Mary had never seen the doctor until that visit. After the doctor checked her, he told Mary it would be a couple of weeks to a month before she was going to deliver, and that she should go home. Lil drove Mary and Mark back to the trailer.

When I got home later that day, Mary said her contractions were coming about ten minutes apart, and she wanted to go to the hospital. We called Mike Gehm's wife, Mary, and asked her to watch Mark while I took my Mary to the hospital. She came over right way, and we took off, with Mark crying in the background because he wanted his mommy and he didn't want her to leave. Things worked out just fine, as Mary was in the hospital when Eric was born at 10:16 on March 12, 1969. He weighed six pounds nine ounces and was nineteen inches long. I took a few days off to stay with Mark until Mary came home from the hospital. Her sister Marge flew in from Detroit to help for about a week. Mark and I went to the airport in Duluth to pick her up and bring her back to Grand Marais.

We adapted quite well to the circumstances of a new baby, in a new home, in a new town, and a new job at the Coast Guard Station. It was a bit hard on Mary as we didn't have another car. She would drop me off at work every day and come to pick me up after work. This was difficult for her with two little kids to transport, though our laundry was done at the station. I could use their washer and dryer to save us time and money. I got real good at folding clothes especially cloth baby diapers. We weren't able to travel to Duluth to go shopping at the Duluth Air Force Base commissary anymore as it was too far away. We bought all of our groceries in town at the local grocery stores at tourist prices. There never was enough money to go around in Grand Marais either.

Eric was a colicky baby and cried all of the time, and I do mean all of the time. He just about drove Mary nuts. Mark who was starting to talk would say, "Shut up, baby. Shut up," as he would give him his pacifier to quiet him down, but that didn't

Above: Mike, Mark, Mary, and Eric in our trailer at Grand Marais in March 1969. (Photo Mike Roberts)

At left: Mark and Eric, July 1969. (Photo Mike Roberts)

work for very long as he just spat it out and start crying again. Eric eventually got over the colic at about five months of age and turned out to be a very contented, happy child. Mark was ever glad that he did. They became playmates and the best of friends.

COAST GUARD PEOPLE AT NORTH SUPERIOR LIFEBOAT STATION AT GRAND MARAIS
March 1969 to February 1970

THE PEOPLE I RECALL STATIONED at the Grand Marais Coast Guard station at the same time as I was there—March 1969 to February 1970—were the following:

The officer in charge was Chief Boatswain Mate Tom Whalen, his wife, Lil, and their two kids. Chief Whalen was a fair-minded, career-oriented man who was getting close to the end of his twenty years in the service. He had served on many different duty stations and ships during his time in the Coast Guard. The Walens were transferred during the winter of 1969-1970, but I don't recall where they went. I hated to see them go.

Chief Engineman Tom Willis was a first-class petty officer when he came to North Superior from Alaska and was promoted to chief shortly after his arrival. He came off a ship there before he came to the Grand Marais lifeboat station. There was no billet for a chief engineman, so he was transferred while I was there, but, again, I can't recall where he went.

Second Class Engineman Jerry Gaillard was at Grand Marais the entire time I was stationed there. His home was Shaker Height, Ohio, a wealthy suburb of Cleveland. Jerry was a great guy who was in love with all of the girls in town, and they loved him too. He was a handsome heartbreaker, a good mechanic, and an all-around nice guy.

Seaman Orrie Holman was from Golden, Colorado, and just about at the end of his four-year enlistment. He too had been stationed in Alaska prior to his arrival in town and wanted to go back as a civilian to travel down the Yukon River from its source in the Northwest Territories of Canada to it's Kuskokwim Bay termination in the Bering Sea. He talked about all of the wildlife he had seen during his Alaskan tour and wanted to go back there. He was a runner and physical fitness enthusiast who trained all of the time for his future adventures in the wilds of our fiftieth state.

Seaman Bruce Bendinger was an idealistic young guy who had just graduated from boot camp. I don't recall his home of record, but he had many hobbies, one of which was cutting out the outline of the presidents heads on U.S. coins with a fine tooth jewelers saw and making jewelry out of them. He taught me how to do it while we were stationed together there. When he got out, he wanted to go back to school on the GI bill and study to become a psychologist. He was a nice guy, and I often wonder if he ever went back to school. In my mind's eye, he did get a good education and became successful at whatever he tried.

Seaman Mike Gehm was at the Duluth Lifeboat Station where we were stationed together, before I was transferred to the Split Rock Lighthouse. His Coast Guard service number was one number higher than mine. My service number was 361-424 and his was 361-425. He was also in Grand Marais for a while until he made third-class engineman and was transferred to the Devils Island Light Station in the Apostle Islands near Bayfield, Wisconsin. He got an early out to go to college. When he was finally discharged, he went back to Duluth to get his paper work of final separation. While he was signing the paperwork in the Group Duluth office in the upstairs of the Lifeboat Station, the guys he used to be stationed with there jacked up his Volkswagen and left it on jack stands in the parking lot at the station and wouldn't let it back down until he gave them money for beer. Mike and his wife, Mary, went back to the Green Bay area of Wisconsin, where they had a couple of kids, raised Christmas trees, started and still run several successful businesses. We keep in contact by exchanging annual Christmas cards and an occasional e-mail.

Seaman Curley Rademacher was just getting out of the service about the time I came to Grand Marais. He was going to go back home to Marshall, Minnesota, to become a city policeman there.

Keith Brubaker was stationed at Grand Marais as an engineman third class. He was drowned in the Grand Marais harbor on July 11, 1967, after hitting an obstruction with the station's small boat. He was alone in the boat at the time, fell in and was drowned. The water in Lake Superior is so cold year round that, plunged into the water, it instantly takes the breath away. He was the second Coastguardsman to be killed in the line of duty in Minnesota on Lake Superior during the four years of my Coast Guard enlistment. I did not know him personally but heard the story of his demise when I came to North Superior Life Boat Station at Grand Marais in March of 1969 after Split Rock Lighthouse closed.

There were other guys stationed at North Superior Lifeboat Station in Grand Marais at the time, but I can't recall their names, where they were from, or their circumstances of enlistment and where they went after they got out. Everyone had a story to tell.

DAILY ROUTINE AT NORTH SUPERIOR LIFEBOAT STATION AT GRAND MARAIS

WE STARTED OUR DAY AT NORTH SUPERIOR at 8:00 A.M. every weekday morning. We would gather in the day room, and Chief Whalen, or who ever was in charge, would give out the day's assignments. We were a search-and-rescue unit that had a wooden thirty-six-foot motor life boat as our rescue vessel.

Coast Guard thirty-six-foot motor life boat used on search and rescue like the one used in Grand Marais, Minnesota. (Photo Robert Proseus. Used by permission)

We had rotating duty, so that, every so many days, each of us had to stand an overnight watch. While on watch, like at the Duluth Life Boat Station, we monitored the radios, ran the teletype and answered the telephone. When standing the watch, it started after evening chow and went until 8:00 A.M. the next morning. Grand Marais was only a six- to eight-man station, so we didn't have a cook. The guys who lived in

Coast Guard Station Grand Marais from the harbor. (Photo Lila Panek. Used by permission)

the upstairs barracks cooked for themselves. There was a galley, and the watch stander had to keep it clean. The watch stander also stripped, washed and waxed the floors once a week after lights out at 10:00 P.M. While on watch, we could be entertained by TV, read and do anything we wanted, but we had to stay near the watch room of the station, so we could hear the radios and answer the phone. We could sleep in the day room on the couch after 10:00 P.M. The single guys had rooms upstairs at the station, and the married guys went home after each day's work unless they had the watch. There were two apartments in the same building as the station, and the officer in charge and his family and a married man with dependents lived in those apartments.

The boat house was not attached to the main building of the station but was a short distance away.

We also had a vehicle garage separate from the other buildings. The truck was parked in the vehicle garage, and there was a wood shop in the front part of it. All of the buildings were heated with oil furnaces.

While standing the watch, we could go outside, but we had to be within hearing of the phone and radios.

I recall being on the front porch of the station while on watch and shooting into the harbor with a wrist-rocket slingshot. Taconite pellets were the ammunition. At Taconite Harbor, the trains came from the Hoyt Lakes mine already pelletized full of taconite pellets to be loaded on the ore boats that docked there. Along the train

North Superior Coast Guard Station in Grand Marais, circa 1951. (Photo Don Severson. Used with permission)

146

North Superior Coast Guard Station in Grand Marais as seen from the harbor, circa 1951. (Photo Don Severson. Used with permission)

tracks many pellets fell out of the train cars on their way to the dock. Every time we'd go under the railroad overpass on Highway 61, I'd stop and pick a three-pound coffee can full of pellets from along the right of way. That can would last me until the next time we went past Taconite Harbor. I got pretty good with the slingshot, and the pellets were just the right size, a little smaller that a marble, but when they hit some thing solid like a rock or tree, they'd shatter into a 1,000 pieces.

North Superior Station Boat House, circa 1951. (Photo Don Severson. Used with permission)

I noticed a slight tide in the harbor. There was a little pond between the breakwall and the harbor that had a culvert in it, and at times the pond would be full of water and others not quite as full. I know everyone told me there was no tide in the Great Lakes, but as an unofficial observer who never really measured it, I think I detected a slight one.

We worked around the station doing the usual Coast Guard maintenance, standing watch, scraping, painting, fixing, mowing the grass, shoveling and blowing snow

Coast Guard Station, Grand Marais in winter from Artists Point. (Photo Mike Gehm. Used with permission)

in the winter. The crew did all of those mundane tasks while waiting for boat calls to come in.

I do recall an instance while blowing snow out by the garage, when the snow blower picked up a rock and threw it through the garage window about fifty feet away. Opps, I didn't have to pay for it, but I did have to replace the broken glass. Working around the station doing all of the tasks that made the place look sharp in the summer and the winter seemed to make the time go faster.

CARVED NAMES IN THE ROCK

DURING MY TENURE AT GRAND MARAIS, we had to go out on the breakwall to check the lighthouse at the end of it. It stood on legs and rose about twenty-five or thirty feet above the water. It was automated, so there was nothing that needed doing; we just inspected it from time to time.

After one such inspection, I climbed down off of the breakwall and walked the rock back toward the station and Artists Point. When I got just about even with the station, I noticed there were many names and dates etched into the bed rock of the shore. I even found a picture of an old ship there, too. Being a bit of a history buff, that piqued my interest. I wondered who would spend the time and take the trouble to carve their names in that hard rock. Some of the carvings were very elaborate, almost like the work done on tombstones. Most of the names and dates were from around the late 1800s, and their home towns varied. I asked the guys at the station about it, but no one had seen them nor were they very interested either. From time to time, I would walk the rocks and look at the names and dates, wondering who put them there and why. One bright sunny day in the early summer of 1969, I stopped in at the Backlund Hardware store downtown to buy something, and Mr. Backlund was sitting in the window catching some sun and watching the tourists go by. I had seen him sitting in the window many times before, and he always waved at me. Not flamboyantly, mind you, but just a finger or two raised in recognition. We said hello, and he asked if he could help me with any thing. I said yes, but not with hardware just then. I asked him if he would answer some questions I had about the town and the rock carvings.

He had another chair close by and said, "Pull up a chair," and motioned for me to sit down. He was a really old guy probably in his middle to late eighties and said that he'd run the hardware store for years. As we talked, he mentioned that he had some sons who were now in the construction business in town. They had thought a lot about the bad economy and were going to quit to do something else as it was hard to make a living in building at that time. A church job in town came up, so they bid it outrageously high, their plan being that they would either going to make some money this time or quit the business if they didn't get the bid. They got the contract and that kept them going.

I asked him about the carved names in the rock near the breakwall, and he said that around the turn of the century or a little before, visitors used to come to town on ships for vacation. There wasn't much to do around town, so they spent their time on the shore carving their names in the rock. Some vacation. I cross-checked this rock carving explanation with another old guy, Ed Jackson, who lived in a small shack next to the trailer park. Mark and I went to visit him from time to time, and he told me the same story as Mr. Backlund. To be sure that the information was accurate, I also asked Bill Bally, Sr., about the carvings, and he told the same story as the other two guys. There are many names and dates recorded there. I always thought it might be a neat idea to catalogue the carvings as to location and content and write up a pamphlet about it for the tourist's information, but the road to hell is paved with good intentions and, as of yet, I haven't done it. Maybe at some time in the future, when I'm looking for something to do in my retirement, I'll go back to Grand Marais to photograph and catalog these representations of summertime visits by tourists of long, long ago.

Waves crashing to shore at Artist Point in Grand Marais. (Photo Lila Panek. Used with permission)

BALLY THE BLACKSMITH OF GRAND MARAIS

Bally the blacksmith's shop was the place to have major mechanical things repaired in Grand Marais. During our one-year stay in town, I had to have a few things welded up for the Coast Guard Station. I stopped in at their shop many times on the hillside below Highway 61, which is now is registered on the list of Historic Places. .

Bill Senior was a spry old guy in his late eighties who had lots of stories to share about his and Grand Marais's colorful past. He talked of lumberjacks and logging camps to commercial fishermen and the wooden boats they used in days gone by. He had a great memory for things of the good old days and was willing to share them. He was in good shape for his advanced age and was at the shop most of the time

Bill, Jr., was a college educated engineer who, after graduation, chose to come back and help his dad run the blacksmithing business. Bill, Jr., did the physical work—the lifting, welding and wrenching in the repair shop that catered to fixing the break downs of the loggers and their trucks and skidders. Bill, Sr., did the non-physical side of the business, mostly customer relations. He came in every day and said it got him out of the house. They liked us Coastguardsmen at the blacksmith shop, as we always had a few stories of our own to add to the on going conversations around the barrel stove and coal-fired forge. They always had time to talk.

Bill, Jr., had a complete machine shop with lathes, shapers, grinders, and the like set up in a separate metal building behind the blacksmith shop. He always said if the blacksmith shop ever burned down, at least it wouldn't get his machines. They had a barrel stove that burned used oil to heat the shop. A five-gallon bucketful of old oil was hung on the nearby wall, elevated a foot or so above the barrel, had a valve on it and was piped a few feet over to the top of the stove. The copper tubing from the bucket went through a hole in the top of the stove, and the oil dripped down in to an angle iron capped off on one end and stood at an angle on the bottom of the stove. When the drop of oil hit the hot angle iron, it would pool and burn. The wider the valve was opened, the more oil got fed to it, the hotter the barrel got. Sometimes it would be so hot that the sides of the barrel would be a cherry red. It was a cheap and efficient way to heat the shop, but they didn't trust the safety of it. Whenever they left the shop for any length of time and no one was around, they shut the valve off, and the fire would go out. When they came back, they would relight it, and, in a short time, it would be blazing hot in there again.

Bill, Jr., could do just about anything that needed doing along the heavy repair or replacement line, and, if he couldn't fix it or reproduce it, he would order it from one of his many sources somewhere, and it usually would be on the next bus to town. Bill, Sr., and Bill, Jr., were very nice guys, a credit to the town, worked together well and got along with everyone—townies, Coasties, loggers, and tourists alike. They were real true characters, and the town was better for them being there to fix whatever was broken.

During the winter of 1969-1970, I had brought my 8-N tractor over to Bally's shop to have some welding done on the bucket. I was due to get out of the service in April of 1970 when my enlistment was up, and I needed to get the tractor over to the home place in Ely eighty miles away. Bill, Jr., knew I was getting out soon, so one day he asked me how I planned to get the tractor over to Ely. I told him I might drive it there, and he said it was an awful long way to drive a tractor. I asked him if he had any ideas on how to solve problem of getting the tractor back to Ely. He said, yes, he did. He was going to go to Duluth soon to pick up some steel and coal for the blacksmith business, then pick up his girlfriend and give her a ride back to Grand Marais. He said, if I paid for his gas and helped him load the steel and coal and help drive when he got sleepy, he would load up the tractor on his truck and deliver it to Ely on his way to Duluth. It would be a long day, but it was a great solution to the problem of getting the tractor back to Ely.

We loaded and secured the tractor on the flat-bed truck the night before to save time the next day. He picked me up at 3:00 A.M., and we headed for Ely. It was an uneventful trip, but when we got there, we found that we couldn't unload the tractor at my mother's place in Winton because there was no loading ramp. We went to Ely and found a place to get it off the truck. It was so cold, and we had a devil of a time getting the tractor started. It had a six-volt electrical system, and it was always a hard starter. After quite a while and a couple of cans of ether later, it finally popped off, and we unloaded it. It was still too far to drive the tractor to Winton if we wanted to get back to Grand Marais at a descent hour, so we left it in Ely.

We got back on the road without further delay, as it was a good two-hour trip to Duluth. We finally arrived, loaded up the steel and coal and headed up Highway 61 towards Two Harbors. We picked up Bill's girlfriend on the way and kept going north up the shore as it was getting dark. In Beaver Bay, we stopped for gas. After filling up, Bill asked if I would drive the rest of the way home as he was getting very tired, and he could hardly keep his eyes open anymore. I said, "Sure," and got in the drivers seat while he rode shotgun.

Bill's girl was sitting in the middle between us. I had never driven his truck before but started out in low gear from the lighted up gas station. As the truck started to get up to speed, the time to shift to the next higher gear was signaled by the whine of the engine. The inside of the cab was now pitch black. I stepped on the clutch and reached for the gear shift knob. Instead, I grabbed Bill's girl by the leg right close to the knee. She let out a scream, which scared the hell out of me. Bill, who was getting ready to nod off, hollered, "What's going on over there"? I apologized for grabbing her leg and shifted in to the next gear. We all had a good laugh and drove off into the night, heading for Grand Marais. It was a long day.

WORKING AT THE HOLIDAY IN GRAND MARAIS
April, May & June 1969

THE HOLIDAY STATION STORE IN Grand Marais was not a company store but was owned by a franchisee name Mike. He was a local guy who had started his station store as an Ericson station, and when Ericson became Holiday, he too took the Holiday name. In those days, the stations had gas pump attendants who pumped the gas for customers. I pumped gas, and he ran the inside store. It worked well until the tourist season got under way. Then it became too much for me to stand watch and work at the Coast Guard station and then go to work at Holiday, too. After a while, I just couldn't do it on an everyday basis so I gave my notice and quit. Mike understood my situation, was good about it and said if I wanted to come back to work to just give him a call and he'd see what he could do.

WORKING OTHER JOBS IN GRAND MARAIS
March 1969 to February 1970

AFTER WE CAME TO GRAND MARAIS and settled in, we needed more money, and the Coast Guard just wasn't supplying it for us. The costs to live there were much more than at Split Rock, and we were, to say the least, shocked. We now had to pay heat, lights, phone, and lot rental, and there was too much month left at the end of the paycheck. I went to work part time and did many jobs while there. I got a job pumping gas at Holiday with the good recommendation from the Two Harbors Holiday, but that didn't make a dent in what it cost to live in Grand Marais. I shoveled snow off roofs and plowed snow in the winter, painted Joe Thompson's cabins at the trailer park in the summer. I helped renovate a wood business's shop and sided a sawmill building in the fall. While doing all of these side jobs, I also worked at the local phone company as a janitor/handyman.

FLOOD DETAIL IN DULUTH
Spring 1969

OUR JOBS IN THE COAST GUARD were varied but centered on search and rescue. We were part of the armed services, but were under the jurisdiction of the Treasury Department and then the Department of Transportation on a national level, which made our service unique. We served in many capacities, which were ever expanding. One of these services was flood detail. In the springtime, after a winter of lots of snow, when it started to melt, the creeks and rivers overflowed their banks. One area of high water and flooding was the Dakotas and North Dakota in particular. The Red River of the North runs into the Hudson Bay and forms the western border of Minnesota and the eastern borders of North and South Dakota as it starts as the Bois De Sioux River near Browns Valley, Minnesota, and becomes the Red River as it flows northward.

If the spring was gradual and the snow melted slowly, it was usually not a problem. The water in creeks and rivers rose but stayed within its banks. However, if spring came

En2 Jerry Gaillard near the Knife River on the way to Duluth for flood detail. (Photo Mike Roberts)

in fast and the weather warmed up quickly, the snow turned into raging creeks, roaring rivers, and lots of trouble for the people living near them. When the water got high and jumped the banks, people got stranded and needed help. They called in the mobile rescue teams of the Coast Guard. During the winter of 1968-1969, we got a lot of snow. When spring time finally arrived, it came fast. Floods looked inevitable. Group Duluth got ready. They called in a couple of guys from each of the outlaying stations to come to Duluth with their small boats on trailers prepared to go out to the Fargo area to help the local authorities rescue stranded residents. Second-Class engineman Jerry Gaillard and I were the men sent from North Superior Life Boat station to be part of the rescue efforts

Mike Gehm from the Grand Marais station had been sent in years past, and he said it was probably the scariest thing he'd ever encountered. The water was high and the current swift, and he feared for his life while on search-and-rescue missions on more than one occasion. When we were sent on a rescue assignments, we couldn't pick the circumstances. We just went and helped out the best you could. The Life Saving Service had a motto: "You have to go out, but you don't always come back." That was what Jerry and I were prepared to do—to go out and hopefully come back. He and I and a bunch of other Coastguardsmen from the area gathered at Duluth to wait for the call to head west with all our rescue equipment. We waited and waited with a close eye on the North Dakota weather reports. We worked around the Coast Guard station to break up the monotony of waiting and played softball for one whole day to kill time waiting for the call to mobilize. I threw my right arm out that day and haven't been able to throw a snow ball over handed ever since. Jerry and I went up town in our dress blues one night and had a couple of beers at the American Legion. The old guys there wouldn't let us buy any drinks. They were happy we came to their club and that we were going on flood detail to North Dakota to rescue people there.

We stayed in Duluth at the ready for about a week, and the call never came in to mobilize to the west. So the rescue groups disbanded, and we traveled back to our

Mike Roberts and Jerry Gaillard standing next to Coast Guard trucks in convoy waiting for orders to go to North Dakota on flood detail. (Photo Mike Roberts)

respective stations, bored as we waited for the call and wanting to help but weren't needed. We were also a bit relieved because it was dangerous duty. Mary and the kids were very happy to see me upon my return to Grand Marais. They said I was gone for a long time, and they missed me.

LOGS IN THE HARBOR
Summer 1969

ON THE WAY TO THE COAST GUARD STATION from town was a narrow strip of land. On the left or east was the lake and on the right or west was the harbor. During the winter, Consolidated Paper Company out of Ashland, Wisconsin, piled pulp logs along the edge of the harbor. They were quite high and a few logs deep. They hauled the 100-inch pulp sticks on both sides of the harbor all winter long. They had a crane with a clam bucket there to off load the logs from the pulp trucks and their pup trailers if they weren't self-unloaders and put them in great parallel piles lining the harbor. All winter long, they hauled the logs from everywhere, truck load after truck load.

When spring came and the ice melted, the paper company brought in a small tugboat to hook on to the large log boom piled on the ground on the west side of the harbor near the west breakwall. They dropped the boom into the harbor log by log and connected them together with chains. After the boom was complete, they began dumping the logs from the harbor shore into the inside of the boom. When the log boom was full, they hooked it to the small tug, and it pulled the logs out of the harbor between the two breakwalls into the lake. Consolidated Paper Company had a bigger tugboat come over from Ashland, pulling a larger log boom behind it.

They took the small boom from inside the harbor and hauled it into the large boom out in the lake. When the big boom was filled from the logs of many small booms, the large tug pulled the big boom over to Ashland in the end of Chequamegan Bay to be processed into paper. It was said that the large boom could haul as much as 4,000 cords of pulpwood at a time. The rafting of logs by Consolidated Paper Company started in 1944 and ended in 1971, the year after we left Grand Marais. This booming method of transporting logs was done for many years. Moving the logs by water was the cheapest way to get them from the woods to the paper mill.

In the early 1950s, logs were loaded on an LST converted to transporting logs by water. The LST had a crane mounted on it and loaded the logs on to the deck of the ship. They were brought to Ashland, Wisconsin, for processing into paper.

Logs being loaded with a crane onto a boat in the Grand Marais harbor, circa 1951. (Photo Don Severson. Used with permission)

156

LOUIE'S PASSING AWAY
July 9, 1969

Mary's father, Louis Fodor, died on July 9, 1969, and we flew to Detroit the next day to attend the funeral. It was a very sad time, as he was only fifty-three years old and had two little kids still at home. Mary handled her father's passing as well as could be expected. We had two little children of our own to take care of, which Mary did with much grace and concern. Eric was a very colicky baby and just about drove everyone nuts with his constant crying. However, when we flew to Detroit, something inexplicable happened on the flight, whatever was making him cry cleared up, and he became the most happy and contented little guy any parent could ask for. Go figure. When we got there, we helped as much as we could with the arrangements and everything went as scheduled.

I had taken ten days of emergency leave for us to attend the funeral and be with Mary's family. When the leave was almost up, we were not finished with all of the things we needed doing. Mary's mother did not drive, so I took her around to all of the places to get the things done that needed doing such as picking out a headstone for Louie, going in to get his tools and clothes from work. I could see that I was going to need more time to finish all of the things that needed to be done.

I called the Grand Marais Station to get an extension on my emergency leave, but they refused my request. I called the Red Cross to see if they could help me get the extension. They told me there was nothing they could do to help me, and I should return to the station on time. I had more than sixty days of leave on the books that the service owed me as I hadn't taken very much leave prior to this emergency. I called the Coast Guard again and requested the extension a second time. They again refused my extension request and told me I'd have to be back before the leave expired or else I'd suffer the consequences.

Everyone in the family got our heads together to see how we could solve this dilemma and get the leave extended. Mary's mom said she knew the priest at the Holy Cross Catholic Church in the Delray section of Detroit. He, apparently, knew everyone. She gave him a call, explained the situation and that she needed help. He said he'd see what he could do. Well, Father Jacob knew Congressman Dingle from Detroit personally and gave him a call to see if he could help us, and help he did. I got two calls from the Red Cross that very day to tell me that they were so happy that they were able to get me as much time as I needed to help Mary tie up the loose ends of her family bereavement. That was an eye opener for me. "It ain't what you know; it's who you know," was a saying my mother used for many years. Damned if she wasn't right on. When it came time for us to go back to Grand Marais, we talked Mary's mom into taking the family car and driving back to Minnesota with us. I did all of the driving and took the circle route around Lake Superior through Canada and got back to Grand Marais just in time for the Fisherman's Picnic.

After the picnic was done, they stayed for another week or so, and my brother Rob came over to Grand Marais from Ely to drive Mary and her two kids back to Detroit. After a few days of visiting my sister Fran there, he took the bus back to Ely. I took the bus from Grand Marais down to Duluth to pick up our car, which we had left in the Coast Guard Lifeboat Station's parking lot and drove it back home up the shore. It was a busy summer.

HUGE WAVES ON SEARCH AND RESCUE
Summer 1969

In mid-summer of 1969, a boat call came in early one morning, and I was on duty as part of the boat crew. We were notified by land line phone that there was a small boat missing over in the Keweenaw Peninsula of Upper Michigan. We were called upon to look for any traces of the vessel. A family consisting of a man, his wife, and a small child were overdue from Isle Royal. They'd boarded their twenty-one-foot boat in the Copper Country and went to Isle Royal on a summer holiday. They vacationed there for about a week or so, and then headed back to the Upper Peninsula. Their parents became alarmed when they didn't show up back in Michigan when they were supposed to. Their folks called the Michigan State Police and asked them to check to see if their children's car and boat trailer was still in the parking lot. The police investigated the request and found that the vehicle and trailer were still there. The police then notified the Coast Guard, and a search got underway. We were part of that search.

The authorities thought they might have gotten lost or turned around and gone the wrong way. We, on our side of the lake, were asked to patrol the shore from Grand Marais to the Canadian border. We were to look for any sign of the boat or people. A life jacket, cooler, an oar or anything that might give a clue as to their fate. The boat crew of the thirty-six footer that went out that morning as Coxswain, Chief Boatswain Mate Tom Whalen, Chief Tom Willis as engineman, and me as seaman and the third crew member. When we left the Grand Marais harbor that morning, the lake was a little choppy with a stiff wind blowing from the southwes—a typical day on Lake Superior. We followed the shore line up toward Grand Portage looking for any flotsam that might indicate it came from the missing boat. That southwest wind produced a following sea, meaning that the waves were pushing the thirty-six footer from behind.

We pulled into he dock at the National Monument Fort of Grand Portage to stretch our legs and ask a few questions to see if anyone had seen any sign of the craft we were seeking. After a short while, we got under way again going past the remote light on Hat Point and past the ancient witches tree there. As we continued up the shore, the wind started to pick up, and the size of the waves increased. It was getting kind of rough, and we were getting bounced back from the waves, hitting the shore and coming back out into the lake. As we traveled toward the border and the Pigeon River, the waves grew even bigger as the wind increased, and it was getting a bit rougher. We weren't too worried, as we weren't very far from shore in case we got in trouble.

The thirty-six-foot Coast Guard Motor Lifeboat was a double-ended vessel with points on both ends. It had a heavy keel, which made it self-righting. If it ever over-turned, it would come back with the cab and wheel on top. The boat was said to be self-bailing and supposedly unsinkable. It was made of wood but also very heavy, which would send us right to the bottom if we took on a lot of water. We rounded the Point and sailed into the mouth of the Pigeon River, the international border between the United States and Canada, and we weren't going any farther up the lake so our search was at an end.

We looked around the river, and then started back out in to the lake. When we rounded the point and traveled the shore toward Grand Marais, the wind was blowing harder and the waves had gotten much bigger. But now they were pounding into us. It was getting rougher and scarier. The two chiefs thought that if we went out a ways in to the lake, the waves might be smaller because they couldn't bounce back from the shore. To find calmer water away from the shore, we went out about two miles out, cutting diagonally across the waves and then resumed our southwesterly course toward home.

I thought that this was one of the dumbest ideas I have ever been witness to, as the wind had really started to blow, and the waves were now approaching gigantic. We would ride a wave up to the top and go over the crest and then go down the wave to the bottom of the trough. The nose of the boat would plow into the oncoming wave and the thirty-six footer would start to climb back up the next wave. As we traveled up the wave to the top, we were in a laid-back position, and the engine was straining all of the way to the top. When we reached the top, the nose of the boat came over and headed down toward the bottom of the trough again. As we started toward the bottom of the trough, the propeller came out of the water with a sputter. On the top of the cowling, which covered the front of the boat, was fog bell. It was a small bell rung at intervals whenever we were in a fog so as to make a clanging noise for identi-fication. Other boats would know we were there and would not run in to us. When we started to come down the wave heading for the trough, the bell would ring once with a ding. When coming out of the trough and heading up the wave, the fog bell would ring again, *ding*. When reaching the top of each wave, we could see for a long way around us. Then down to the bottom of the trough we would go with a *ding* from the bell. When we got to the bottom before we started up the wave again, we were surrounded by water, a huge wall of water in front of us and a huge wall of water behind us. There was water everywhere. The nose of the boat dug into the wall of the water at the bottom of the trough. When climbing the waves, we felt as if we were going to tip over backwards. When we reached the top, the thirty-six footer would hang there for a few seconds, *sputter, sputter* when the prop came out of the water. So we labored for a long, long time. *Sputter, sputter, ding*, and *ding*.

I wanted to stop in at Grand Portage on the way back and said so but Chief Whalen said, "I think it starting to let up." I thought it was getting worse. We even strapped ourselves in with the safety harnesses. If we got washed over the side, we didn't have a snowball's chance in hell of living to the end of the day. We went past Grand Portage and were two miles out, *sputter, sputter ding, ding, sputter, sputter, ding, ding*. I knew when we were out there, fighting those huge waves, I would never see my Mary and my two little boys again in this life. I feared we would never make it back alive. We kept traveling two miles out all of the way back toward Grand Marais. When we finally saw Five Mile Rock, and we hadn't capsized or sunk, I though maybe

Split Rock Lighthouse as seen from the charter boat, the *Grandpa Woo III*, summer 2006. (Photo Mike Roberts)

The charter boat *Grandpa Woo III* loading passengers at the dock in East Beaver Bay for a sight-seeing tour of Split Rock Lighthouse and the Reserve Mining docks in Silver Bay. My last boat ride on Lake Superior in August 2006. (Photo Mike Roberts)

this wasn't my day to die. When we eventually got back into the harbor, away from the high waves and ice-cold water, I was so happy to make it back to dry land again.

That was my last boat call while in the service, and I was ever so glad to live to tell about it. I have only gone for a *Grandpa Woo* (a passenger boat out of East Beaver Bay) boat ride on Lake Superior once after that experience, and, if I can help it, I will never venture out on that killer lake ever again.

They never found hide nor hair of that young couple and their child. To this day as far as I know, they're still missing. "Lake Superior it's said never gives up its dead" according to the song "The Wreck of the Edmund Fitzgerald" by Gordon Lightfoot, and I believe it. They don't find many that are lost on this treacherous inland sea.

GRAND MARAIS'S FISHERMAN'S PICNIC
Summer 1969

THE TOWN OF GRAND MARAIS was pretty sleepy and laid back in 1969-1970 for most of the year, but it came to life during the town's annual celebration, the Fisherman's Picnic. It was held around the end of July, the beginning of August. A carnival came to town with all the thrill rides, food stands, and games of chance that were hawked along the midway. They had a parade, played bingo and, in the evenings, had fireworks. A platform was built next to the Coast Guard station near the breakwall. From there, they shot the fireworks over the harbor.

It was a time of great fun and excitement, and people came from all over the region to attend. They even had a couple of parachutists who landed on the strip of land going out to the Coast Guard station and Artists Point. That must have been a hoot for those guys to land there because it had a power line on that very narrow neck of ground between the lake and the harbor. One false move or too much wind in either direction, and they would be in the ice-cold water or fried by the power line. The picnic celebration lasted for about three days or so, and it was great fun for everyone. What an exciting time for an otherwise sleepy little town way out in the middle of nowhere.

WORKING AT THE PHONE COMPANY
Summer 1969

THE MAIN PART-TIME JOB I had while in Grand Marais was for the Northwestern Bell Telephone Company. A neighbor, who lived in the trailer park and worked for the phone company, mentioned that they were looking for someone to be a part-time janitor/handyman. They had small jobs around the main company building in town and some small jobs out in the outlying switching stations on the shore. I applied for the job and got it. It consisted of the mowing the grass, cleaning the offices and switching station in town and a few other small jobs. I also replaced missing or damaged phone books and the broken glass window panels in the phone booths, up and down the shore. Cleaning the Tofte Switching Station was a weekly or bi-weekly task depending on how much work was done there by the technicians.

It was a great job. The people were nice, and I could work around my Coast Guard schedule. They gave me the keys to the place with the job assignments and let me work at my own pace. It worked out well, and the pay wasn't half bad either. I had an interesting experience while working down in Tofte. The telephone technicians who worked at the Tofte switching station knew there was someone hired to clean up from time to time. They would throw the plastic wire coating scraps after stripping the wire on the floor. That was just fine with me as I had some thing to clean up, there were also waste baskets to empty, floors to sweep, and a few other jobs that generated waste. When I was finished, I would gather up all of the trash and take it up to the local dump on my way home.

The dump was on the back road, up the hill, away from the lake shore. Whoever was in charge of the dump—township or county—would bring in a back hoe and dig a trench about six to eight feet deep, twenty-four inches wide and a couple of hundred feet long or so. All of the dump users seemed to know the drill—they would throw their refuse in the trench. When the trench was full, the back hoe operator would push all the garbage left on top into the ditch, and then dig another trench alongside the old one and cover up the original trench now full of garbage with the dirt from the newly dug trench. They had been disposing of the trash in the landfill for many years this way and it still seemed to be working well.

Where we have garbage and refuse out in the country, we most always have bears. They also know the drill. Bringing garbage to the landfill is like ringing the dinner bell for the bears, and they come for the feast of rotting garbage, fish guts, and other tasty bear snacks. Most of the time, they came at night, but on rare occasions, they would show up during the day. When the people came to throw their trash away, if they saw bears, it was usually not a problem. The dump users would give the bears a wide berth and keep their eye on them. Most of the time that is. When I came to the dump that day, there was one other car there—a city mom with a couple of young kids. I could tell that she wasn't a local as she was dressed to the nines and had a big fancy car, neither practical in country living.

As I was throwing my garbage from the substation into the trench, this woman was trying to get her oldest boy about five or six years old to feed a bear out of his hand so she could take a picture of junior feeding the bear. I couldn't believe anyone could be so dumb and reckless. I asked her what she was doing, and she said trying to get a picture of her son feeding the bear. I asked her if she was nuts or what? I asked if she didn't know that the bear was wild and would eat her and her kids too, if given half a chance. She said no they wouldn't. The little boy was crying, "I don't want to feed the bear. I'm scared." And she was telling him the bears were friendly, and they wouldn't hurt him.

I told her she was going to get her boy killed, and she said that I should mind my own business. I walked back to my car, got in and drove away, absolutely amazed at how a grown woman with kids could be so dumb. I read the local paper to see if the bear killed any of them, and, again, as in other instances, "No news is good news." I guess the boy got to go back home after the vacation was done to do "Show and Tell" at his school and tell how his mom took the picture of him hand feeding the wild bear in the dump up in Tofte.

DEAD CAT
Summer 1969

DURING THE SUMMER OF 1969, I was standing watch on a beautiful evening, the sun was starting to sink in the western sky. I happened to look out the window of the watch room toward the harbor. There in the water about twenty feet of from shore, I thought I could see a round shape of a human head. The hair on the head would part and come back together again as the current of the wind moved the water just a little in small waves. When the hair on the head parted, I could see the white scalp beneath it. There was a drop off, or so it was said, just off from the shore where the head was located.

There was a glare on the water from the setting sun going down. It was hard to see exactly what it was from the window, so I went outside to get a better look from the porch, but still couldn't quite make out what it was. I knew the guy's legs had to hitting the edge of the drop off and that's what kept him from drifting in to the shore. He wasn't drifting out nor coming in to shore but just staying in one spot. It was starting to get a little dark out, so I had to do something soon before all of the daylight was gone. I asked one of the guys watching TV in the day room to listen to the radios for distress calls while I went to the boat house and got a boat hook. It was a long pole with a steel hook on the end to grapple things at a distance in the water.

I reached out and gently hooked the head and tried to maneuver it into shore. I finally got it to move in toward me. Much to my surprise, when I got it close enough to see, it was a dead cat that had bloated up to the size of a human head. The hair that was parting with the waves was the fur. I dragged it into shore, got a shovel, scooped it up and took it to the other side of the vehicle garage where I dug a hole and buried it. I was so relieved that it wasn't a human body, just a poor unfortunate cat.

FIFTEEN-MINUTE STATION RECALLS
Summer 1969

THERE WEREN'T VERY MANY people stationed at the Life Boat Station in Grand Marais at any one time, so when there was a boat call, the guys who were off duty were subject to a fifteen-minute recall. The signal to come back to the station, if they couldn't reach someone by phone, was to turn on the fog horn. If a man was off duty, it wasn't foggy out and he heard the fog signal, it meant there was a boat call and now he had to go back to the station as part of the back-up crew. We only had one thirty-six-foot motor life boat to go out on the lake for Search and Rescue, so I had no idea what we were backing up, but that was the rule—when a boat call came in, we went back to the station for duty.

I recall that I had the Fourth of July of 1969 off and wasn't on duty. Mary and I planned a picnic with Mark and Eric, just to get away from the station and our trailer home for the day. We went to a small park along Highway 61 and the shore and had to take a portable telephone with us, just in case there was a boat call. It was so cold that we had to wear jackets. Mary was bound and determined to wear shorts as it was summer, and she hadn't as yet had a chance to wear them, but she soon changed to her jeans before she got too cold. We had a nice time, even if it was unseasonably cold, ate our special picnic lunch, watched the kids play, and no fifteen-minute recall that day.

BURNING THE THIRTY-SIX FOOTER

WHILE I WAS STATIONED AT North Superior Lifeboat Station in Grand Marais, the Coast Guard had a plan to do away with all of the wooden thirty-six-footer motor lifeboats. They were getting very old and not too reliable anymore, according to some sources, having been built between 1937 and 1956. We purposely ran our thirty-six footer aground near the gravel parking lot on the south side of the station. Chief Whalen hired a tow truck/wrecker from a local towing company to come and winch it up onto the shore. When it was sitting on its side in the middle of the parking lot, we stripped everything of value off it. Most of the good stuff that could be salvaged as keepsakes was kept by Chiefs Whalen and Willis. After all of the hardware was stripped from the boat, we sloshed diesel fuel all over the boat inside the cabin and out on the deck and in the bilges. Whalen touched it off with a whoose and, man, did it burn, right down to its weighted brass keel. A couple of days later, after the ashes had cooled off, we picked through them for any scrap metal to be sold for scrap. We raked up the ashes and anything that didn't burn, hauled them to the dump on top of Pincushion Hill. They had sailed another replacement thirty-six footer that was in better shape up from Duluth before we burned the old one. We got rid of one boat but couldn't tell it from the new one except for the identification number painted on the bow.

SHOVELING ROOFS AND PLOWING SNOW
Winter 1969-1970

IN THE WINTER OF 1969-1970, WE HAD a lot of snow, so, to make some extra money, I thought I might shovel off roofs for people. I put an ad in the local paper, and the phone started to ring. I cleaned off many at $35.00 to $40.00 per roof depending on its steepness. I also chipped ice off of the eaves where it froze close to the edge. I had a few close calls falling off, but the snow was deep, and it didn't worry me too much.

There was one roof shoveling job that stood out as being the most difficult. It was a flat roof on a cabin up on Devil's Track Lake. The people called from the Cities and explained exactly where it was located and that I should get there as soon as possible. They were concerned that the snow would cave in the roof if it wasn't shoveled soon. I said okay, and asked them to send the check to me when I was done. As the roof was flat and the snow was a least a couple of feet deep, I had to lift each shovelful up and carry it to the edge to throw it off. What a job! After that one, I doubled my price if a roof was even close to being flat. The people never batted an eye or tried to bargain, they just paid whatever I asked. Looking back, I sold my services way too cheaply, but the money was good for the labor and danger involved. I also met a lot of very nice people.

I bought the 8-N Ford tractor over in Tofte around the first of the year. I had saved up the money from side jobs and found just the right machine that I could use in Ely when I got out of the service. When I bought it, I asked the guy who sold it if there was any kind of warrantee or guarantee on it and he said, "Ya, there was, thirty seconds or thirty feet, whichever came first." He had just overhauled the engine and said that it would outlast me. I drove it home to the trailer park and plowed snow all over town. I made a few bucks with the machine and when we left town, hauled it back to our place in Ely.

GOING OUT WITH BOB & LILA TO LUTSEN
Janurary 1970

OUR NEXT DOOR NEIGHBORS IN THE trailer park, Bob and Lila Panek, sold their trailer home about mid-summer and moved into a house in the middle of town. As winter approached, Bob and Lila asked us if we would like to go out for the night to hear a band at the Lutsen ski resort. Mary and I hadn't been out on the town since we first moved to Split Rock in 1966. We jumped at the chance. I had put a couple of bucks aside from all of my extra jobs I'd been doing, so we had enough money to do it. We got a baby sitter, and Bob drove. We got half in the bag, laughed, told jokes and had a great night out.

On the way back home, we thought we might stop for a bite to eat, but there was nothing open after 11:00 P.M. Bob invited us to go back to their house for steaks.

Framed painting of Split Rock Lighthouse given to Mike Roberts by Mr. Taylor at General Electric Metalurgical Plant in Detroit, March 1970. (Photo Mike Roberts)

Mary and I couldn't recall the last time we had steak, so we agreed immediately. They had some in the freezer and cooked them frozen. We ate, had some more drinks, talked and laughed into the wee hours of the morning. That outing was our one night of fun during the whole year's time we spent in Grand Marais.

GETTING OUT OF THE SERVICE
AND GOING BACK TO ELY
February 1970

W E WERE DUE TO GET OUT OF THE Coast Guard in April of 1970, and we still had about sixty days of unused leave on the books in February. Mary's mom had invited us to come to Detroit for a while and stay with her so she could bond with her two new grandsons. We thought that was a great idea, so I put in for leave from the Grand Marais Lifeboat Station. They promptly denied our leave request, saying that I was a crucial part of the crew at the station and could not be spared. We were closed down for the winter, but, at the time, we were refurbishing the thirty-six footer, and I was a part of the crew working on it. I talked to and pleaded with the chief to just let us go on leave, and they again said no. I called Group Duluth and requested they give me the time off I had coming. They said that they would not countermand the chief's wishes, so the answer was still no.

It didn't look too good for us taking leave and going to Detroit to be with Mary's mother. After I tried every which way to get them to change their minds, all to no avail, Mary got mad and took the initiative and called the Grand Marais station, talked to the chief and got the same no for an answer. She then called Group Duluth and got another no for an answer, just like I did. She really got mad and told them that I had sixty days of unused leave on the books and that I had less time to serve on my enlistment than I had in leave days coming. They still said no. She then said if they wouldn't grant us our leave, maybe after a call to our congressman, they might see their way clear to change their minds and grant us the leave we had coming. They finally saw her point at the mention of talking to our congressman and said they would get the paper work ready, and they did.

We now had to get our trailer from Grand Marais over to Ely, and it was in the middle of winter with a lot of snow. I hired a neighbor in Ely to plow the quarter-mile stretch of road into our place and make a big turn around so I could get the trailer turned around and situated when we got there. I didn't have a truck to pull it, and the driveway company wanted a $1.00 per mile to haul it, so I made a deal with the local fuel oil company to trade the unused fuel in our the trailer's fuel oil tank for the use of their one ton flat-bed trucks for a couple of days. I had to put an electric hook up on the truck to attach to the electric brakes of the trailer and make them operable. I made two wide-load signs out of hardboard, one for the front of the truck and one for the back of the trailer. I also got the wide-load permits from the MNDOT office in Duluth. On the appointed day and time, I hooked onto the trailer, pulled it out of the trailer space and headed out of town toward Ely on Highway 61 with Mary and the kids following behind in the tan Plymouth station wagon.

DD214 Coast Guard Separation from Active Duty Document. (Artifact Mike Roberts)

We went over the hill at Little Marais, heading to Finland and then took Highway 1 to the west toward Ely. It took us awhile to get going, so, just before we reached Murphy City, it was starting to get dark, and our permit was for daylight hours only.

We also ran into a big snowstorm, so it was time to quit for the day. I pulled into the plowed-out parking lot at Murphy City and asked a lady in a nearby house if it was okay to leave the trailer in the parking lot overnight. She said it would be no problem, so we left the truck and trailer there and drove to my mother's place in Winton.

The next day, we came back and got the trailer and hauled it the rest of the way to our place down off of Highway 1 near the Bear Island River. I got the trailer turned around in the plowed-out yard and got it set in the right place, blocked it up and returned the truck to the oil company in Grand Marais. We came back to Ely, got our stuff and stayed another night at my mom's. We left for Detroit early the next morning.

GOING TO DETROIT WHILE ON LEAVE
March & April 1970

IT TOOK US A COUPLE OF DAYS to get to Detroit through all the spring snowstorms. I don't believe we ever came through the Gaylord and Grayling area of the lower peninsula of Michigan in the winter without hitting a snowstorm. I guess it was the lake effect and this time it was no different. We finally got to Detroit where everyone was so happy to see us, Grandma Mary Fodor especially liked the time with her grandsons. After about the first week of hanging around the house, I told Mary I was going to get a job. She was surprised but said that it might be a good idea, as she could see that I was getting restless from just hanging around the house.

I read the newspaper employment ads for the next few days and saw an ad for a pipefitter job at the General Electric Company on Hoover and Eight-Mile Road of Detroit in the Metallurgical Division. It was at a manufacturing plant where they made things out of carbide and also had an Industrial Diamond Manufacturing facility there as well. I applied for the job and was hired after a grueling all-day physical. I just wanted to make enough money so I would be able to take ninety days off of work before I went back to my old job at Reserve Mining Company in the Peter Mitchell taconite mine in Babbitt. I went to work an eight-hour day at the plant on day shift, and it was great. I got a chance to see how they made the carbide studs for studded tires, triangular carbide tool bits used by machinists and balls for the tips of ball point pens. They dropped small pieces of carbide into the liquid from the top of a shot tower and when they reached the bottom, they were perfectly round. I was happy to be working a five-day week and really enjoyed the work.

I witnessed things I never knew existed and was fascinated by all of the processes that they had developed there. The Industrial Diamond part of the plant however was off limits, I'd have to have a security clearance to work there, which I did not. I did however, get the chance to work on the flushometer valves in the men's and women's bathrooms with a plant protection guard standing outside of the door all the while I was there in that restricted area of the plant. They took industrial espionage very seriously at GE, and I didn't get a chance to see any other part of the industrial diamond plant.

We had coffee time at 9:00 A.M. and lunch around noon everyday. I ate with all the guys from the maintenance gang. One day at lunch, a welder by the name of Taylor came in with a large yellow garbage bag under his arm with something flat in it. During lunch, he opened the package up to a picture of Split Rock Lighthouse painted on a piece of hardboard that he had painted from a postcard. He said it would mean a lot to him if I would take it, seeing as how I had been stationed there, and he had never seen the lighthouse except on the postcard. It had come out in one of our lunch conversations that I was still in the Coast Guard and would be getting out soon, and one of my duty stations was at the Split Rock Lighthouse. Mr. Taylor was getting ready to retire and was going to move up to Munising, Michigan, and spend the rest of his life on the south shore of Lake Superior painting land and sea scapes. I often wondered if he did in fact retire to his dream place on the shore. I think he probably did as he was most passionate about it. I took the painting home, and after twenty years or so of it being stored, Mary had it matted and framed for my fifty-second birthday. It has hung in a place of prominence in all of our homes ever since.

At the end of about six weeks in Detroit, I quit the GE job, and we went back to Ely. On the day that I was getting out of the service, April 17, 1979, we went down to Duluth, to the offices of the Coast Guard, Group Duluth, where I was then discharged from active duty. I still had to serve two years in the inactive Coast Guard Reserves, but had no meetings during those next two years.

FINALLY GETTING OUT OF THE SERVICE
April 1970

I HAD ENLISTED IN THE COAST GUARD on April 18, 1966, and served a four-year enlistment. I was released from active duty on April 17, 1970, after serving one day less than four years. Prior to my final release, we went to the Duluth Air Force base so I could still use my military ID card one more time at the commissary. We shopped there like there was no tomorrow. We bought massive quantities of everything we thought we might need for the next ninety days. I had previously bought a freezer from Chief Tom Willis in Grand Marais, and we had brought it to Ely. We filled it with everything, including meat, that could be frozen. We had can goods galore, and it looked like we could feed an army. After this last shopping trip to the Air Force Base, we went to the U.S. Coast Guard Headquarters of Group Duluth located upstairs of the Duluth Lifeboat Station to get my final discharge. All of the paper work was ready to go, and when I signed them, they put me in for a DD-214.

It felt like a huge weight had been lifted from my shoulders. We could now come and go as we pleased, no more fifteen-minute recall, no more port and starboard duty, no more liberty cards and one of the best things of all, no more uniforms. I could wear what-ever I wanted wherever I wanted. It felt so great to be finally out. It took me about one year to get over the nagging feeling that I had to go back. I was automatically enrolled in the inactive reserves for two years to fulfill my six-year service obligation and could be re-called to active duty any time during that time, but they never called me back up. I got my final discharge in the spring of 1972, six years after I had enlisted in 1966.

I had met my life's goal of not being killed while in the service even though I thought my number was up at least once during my military time. We had two won-derful children born to us while I served.

Mary didn't have to be dragged from pillar to post anymore to be with me during my Coast Guard tour. I look back on those years as being interesting, enriching and gratifying. However, if given the chance, I doubt that I would do it again. It took a big chunk of our lives right out of the middle of my top earning years, which can never be gotten back. I'm neither whining nor complaining, as I had great duty during my service time. There were about 58,000 American military personnel who gave their lives during the Vietnam conflict. To this day, I still think we, as a country, made a big mistake by going there. Even our leaders at that time, who were so gung ho about stopping the worldwide spread of communism, now admit in their waning years, that it was a colossal national blunder and all for naught. I sometimes wonder if we as a country learned anything from that experience.

The military draft has disappeared for the time being so no other young people will be forced to serve unwillingly in places so far from home for no other reason than a law that said they had to. I, for one, hope it stays that way.

CHAPTER ELEVEN

CONCLUSION

When I went into the U.S. Coast Guard in the spring of 1966, I had no idea what the outcome would be. The times were unsettling and Vietnam was a real shooting war with the casualties mounting daily. I had only known one guy who had benn in the Coast Guard, and he never had too much to say about it. Enlisting in the military was a family tradition. My dad had been in the Navy during World War II, but for me, it was not a lifelong dream. It was a place to serve a legal obligation to the country which was six years in length at that time. I was fortunate to serve with people who took their obligations seriously, and, during my service time, I knew I could count on any of them to hold up their end of the job.

When writing this book, I called and emailed many of my ex-service mates for pictures, information, and timelines. Not one of them said, "I'm sorry, I can't help you," but all of them said, "What do you need? How can I help you?" That was amazing forty years after being discharged. They wouldn't even let me reimburse them for the postage costs incurred in their mailings.

I have lived in other parts of the country since my discharge from the service in 1970, but everywhere I have been, the consensus has always been the same: the U.S. Coast Guard is a good outfit that saves lives and helps people. I agree. While I did not make the military service my life's work, I look back on the time served on Lake Superior, and I'm happy that, if I had to go in, it was in that branch of the armed services.

Mary and I are proud of our three sons who have all done well in their chosen fields of work. They and their wives have given us seven wonderful grandchildren. For us, looking back, life has come out really well. I have always had work with very interesting jobs and enjoyed them, some more than others. While we never made a lot of money in our life's vocational choices, Mary and I have found something money can't buy, which is family harmony, peace, contentment, and generous amounts of happiness.

APPENDIX

COAST GUARDSMEN OF SPLIT ROCK (1966 TO 1969)

MIKE ROBERTS

MIKE ROBERTS JOINED THE U.S. COAST GUARD on April 18, 1966, went to boot camp in Cape May, New Jersey, and was stationed at the Duluth Life Boat Station from July to December 1966. He and his wife, Mary, were transferred to Split Rock Lighthouse, as it was a two man station and a married seaman was needed to fill the quarters and be an assistant to the officer in charge. He was stationed at Split Rock until it was decommissioned and closed in January 1969. They left Split Rock on March 1, 1969, when he was transferred to the North Superior Lifeboat Station in Grand Marais, Minnesota. He served the remainder of his four-year enlistment at Grand Marais and was discharged from active duty on April 17, 1970. All of his time in the service, with the exception of boot camp, was spent on the north shore of Lake Superior in Minnesota.

Mike Roberts's official boot camp photo. (Photo USCG)

175

Mike went back to Ely and worked at the taconite mine in Babbitt, Minnesota, for six years. When the mine was in danger of closing, he accepted jobs at Jackson and St. Cloud, Minnesota, technical colleges teaching plumbing. He taught for twenty-six years, retired in 2007 and presently lives in rural Central Minnesota near his children and grandchildren. At the suggestion of Mary, his wife of forty-five years, and their three children, Mike has written his recollections of his Coast Guard service days, which are contained in this narrative.

BRUCE ROBB

BRUCE ROBB ENTERED THE U.S. COAST GUARD on August 2, 1965, and was from Des Plaines, Illinois. He came to Group Duluth and the Duluth Life Boat Station following boot camp. After he and Kathy were married in January of 1966, they were

SN Bruce Robb's official Cape May, New Jersey, boot camp photo taken the summer of 1965. (Photo USCG)

transferred to the Superior Entry Light Station in Superior, Wisconsin. When attaining the rank of third-class boatswain mate, he was transferred back to the Duluth Life Boat Station. While at Duluth, he became a second-class boatswain mate. He was called into the Group Duluth office and informed that he was being transferred to Split Rock Light Station as Woodard was being sent to Bayfield, Wisconsin.

Robb came to Split Rock in the fall of 1967 and was the officer in charge for about a year. In the late fall of 1968, Second-Class Boatswain Mate Bruce Robb and First-Class Boatswain Mate Jim Schubert of the Two Harbors Light Station mutualed, that is changed duty stations. Jim and Carol Schubert came to Split Rock Lighthouse, and Bruce and Kathy Robb went to Two Harbors Light Station. Bruce was the officer in charge there until he was discharged from active duty, August 1, 1969. He and Kathy went back to live in the suburbs of Chicago, raised a son, had their own business, and he worked for the State of Illinois. They currently live in the Chicago area and have a home on the Des Plains River.

JIM SCHUBERT

JIM SCHUBERT ENTERED THE U.S. COAST GUARD on May 30, 1966, and completed his boot camp training, July 29, 1966. He was sent to Kodiak, Alaska, and served aboard the

210-foot Coast Guard Cutter *Confidence*, W619, from August of 1966 until February of 1968. While on the ship, he made the rank of third-class boatswain mate. He was then transferred from Alaska to Two Harbors, Minnesota, and was the officer in charge of the Two Harbors Light Station until he mutualed with Second-Class Boatswain Mate Bruce Robb. Jim and his wife, Carol, came to Split Rock Lighthouse in December of 1968. Split Rock Light Station was closed on January 1, 1969, so Jim then went to the Bayfield Life Boat Station in Bayfield, Wisconsin. Jim achieved the rank of E-6, first-class boatswain mate. To make E-6 in less than four years of service was almost impossible to do in the Coast Guard at that time. He received an early discharge in March of 1970, as the Coast Guard

Jim Schubert in his dress blues holding his son, Mike. (Photo Carol Schubert)

was giving early outs to enlistees who wanted to go to college. He attended Southern Colorado State College in Pueblo. In the fall of 1970, the Schuberts went back to the Mineral Point area of Wisconsin to begin farming and raising a family. They have made agriculture their families life's work. As of this writing, Jim Schubert is semi-retired and is considering his future options.

LEON T. WOODARD

LEON "LEN" T. WOODARD WAS A CAREER COASTGUARDSMAN from New Bern, North Carolina. As a young man, he joined the U.S. Coast Guard at Norfolk, Virginia, in 1953 as that was a traditional career path for males from the Atlantic Coastal Region of the South. During his twenty-year service, he was stationed at the following Life Boat Station locations: Colonial Beach, Hatteras Inlet, on the Outer Banks of North Carolina, Oak Island, North Carolina, and Bayfield, Wisconsin, two different times. Leon was a Coast Guard recruiter in Moorhead City, North Carolina, and served on the following ships during his twenty year career: The Coast Guard Cutter *Chincoteague*, Norfolk, Virginia, Coast Guard Cutter *Mendota*, Wilmington, North Carolina, Coast Guard Cutter *Mistletoe*, Portsmouth, Virginia,

Chief Leon Woodard in his khaki uniform in June 1968. (Photo Doris Woodard. Used with permission)

Coast Guard Cutter *Acacia*, Port Huron, Michigan, and Coast Guard Cutter *Laurel*, Moorhead City, North Carolina. He also served at the Coast Guard Reserve Center, Detroit, Michigan, and was a lighthouse keeper at Split Rock Lighthouse, Two Harbors, Minnesota, for four years. He retired from the Service in 1973 at Moorhead City, North Carolina.

He rose through the ranks, was a first-class boatswain mate at Split Rock and made chief boatswain mate after leaving the lighthouse and retired as chief six years later. After his retirement from the Service, he went home to New Bern, North Carolina, and bought a 170-foot shrimp boat and named it the *Lady Doris* after his wife, who traveled with him throughout his career. After shrimping for six years, the boat met with disaster, a fire in the engine room. It burned completely up on the Outer Banks of North Carolina at Oakracoke Island. Leon was later diagnosed with a rare disease, arterial malformation of the spine, confined to a wheel chair for sixteen years and died in 2004. His widow, children, and grandchildren still live in North Carolina.

The shrimp boat Lady Doris, named for Leon's wife and owned by Leon Woodard, docked at Pamilco, North Carolina. It had an engine fire and burned up at Orcracoke, Outer Banks of North Carolina. (Photo Doris Woodard. Used with permission)

ABOUT THE AUTHOR

Mike Roberts lives in rural St. Cloud, Minnesota, with his wife, Mary. They have been married for forty-six years and have three boys who have grown to be outstanding young men with families of their own. Their seven grandchildren bring joy, enthusiasm, and activity into their grandparents' lives.

     Mike is a veteran of the U.S. Coast Guard and served during the Vietnam War era from 1966 to 1970 and spent those four years of military service on Lake Superior. After getting out of the service in 1970, Mike went back to work at Reserve Mining Company in the Peter Mitchell Taconite mine in Babbitt, Minnesota. When rumblings of the mine closing due to pollution issues of Lake Superior came from the federal court system, Mike quit the mine and moved his family to Jackson, Minnesota, where he took a job as a Plumbing instructor in the Jackson Technical College there. Do to a change in the way post-secondary education was delivered and financed, the students stopped enrolling in the plumbing class and school. Mike, the junior instructor in a two-man department, was laid off due to a student to teacher ratio imbalance after teaching in Jackson for thirteen years. He went back into industry for the next six years, which included a job on the East Coast in Delaware and working for a mechanical contractor in Red Wing, Minnesota, on the Mississippi River until a job teaching plumbing opened up at the St. Cloud Technical College in St. Cloud, Minnesota.

Mike, who is a journeyman and master plumber, taught plumbing in St. Cloud for the next thirteen years until his retirement in 2007. He and Mary are now both retired and enjoy their free time doing anything that catches their fancy, which includes going to their grandchildren's spots and school activities. He spends his summers gardening, doing yard work, going to rummage and yard sales with Mary, looking for books and bluegrass records and anything he absolutely can't live without, golfing with his sons and is presently trying to start a vineyard with his son Tim. Life is good and retirement is the job that he has been looking for all his life!